50 Useful Excel Functions

Excel Essentials Book 3

M.L. HUMPHREY

TITLES BY M.L. HUMPHREY

EXCEL ESSENTIALS
Excel for Beginners
Intermediate Excel
50 Useful Excel Functions

WORD ESSENTIALS
Word for Beginners
Intermediate Word

WRITING ESSENTIALS
Writing for Beginners
Excel for Writers

SELF-PUBLISHING ESSENTIALS
Excel for Self-Publishers
AMS Ads for Authors
CreateSpace for Beginners
ACX for Beginners

BUDGETING FOR BEGINNERS
Budgeting for Beginners
Juggling Your Finances Basic Excel Primer
Juggling Your Finances Basic Math Primer

CONTENTS

Introduction	1
How Formulas and Functions Work	3
Where To Find Functions	7
Formula and Function Best Practices	13
Copying Formulas	17

EXCEL FUNCTIONS

SUM	19
PRODUCT	21
SUMPRODUCT	23
AVERAGE	25
AVERAGEA	27
MEDIAN	29
MODE	31
MODE.SNGL	33
MODE.MULT	35
MIN	39
MINA	41
MAX	43
MAXA	45
ROUND	47
ROUNDUP	49
ROUNDDOWN	51

COUNT	53
COUNTA	55
COUNTBLANK	57
COUNTIF	59
COUNTIFS	61
SUMIF	63
SUMIFS	65
AVERAGEIF	67
AVERAGEIFS	69
UPPER	71
LOWER	73
PROPER	75
LEFT	77
RIGHT	79
MID	81
TRIM	83
CONCATENATE	85
TEXT	87
TODAY	91
NOW	93
IF	95
VLOOKUP	99

AND	103	*RANK.AVG*	121
OR	105	*SMALL*	123
TRUE	107	*LARGE*	125
FALSE	109	**Other Functions**	127
NA	111	**Combining Functions**	129
RAND	113	**When Things Go Wrong**	131
RANDBETWEEN	115	**Conclusion**	135
RANK	117	**Appendix A: Cell Notation**	137
RANK.EQ	119	**Alphabetical Listing of Functions Covered**	139

INTRODUCTION

In *Excel for Beginners* and *Intermediate Excel* I focused on how to use Excel to perform the tasks a user would need to know on a daily basis. In *Excel for Beginners* the focus was on entering information into Excel, formatting it properly, performing some basic analysis, and then printing the results. In *Intermediate Excel* it was on taking the analysis you can do in Excel to the next level using pivot tables, charts, and conditional formatting as well as some other data manipulation tricks I've found useful over the years.

And while I did cover certain functions in those books. Specifically, SUM and PRODUCT in *Excel for Beginners* and CONCATENATE, IF, COUNTIF/COUNTIFS, SUMIF/SUMIFS, and TEXT in *Intermediate Excel*, I didn't spend a large amount of time on functions in those books because the type of functions users will need are different.

I, for example, love to use SUMIFS and build nested IF functions. But it's possible another user would never use either one of those but might find a function like UPPER, which puts text into upper case letters, incredibly useful.

I didn't want to bog down either of those books with a discussion of functions that most users wouldn't use. However, as I was making the video course versions of those books it occurred to me that there was room to explore functions in more detail.

That's what this book will do. It covers the fifty most useful Excel functions. (In my opinion. Others would probably have a different list.) There are functions related to text, statistics, math, dates, information, and logic, so it's a little bit of everything.

For those of you who've already read *Excel for Beginners* and *Intermediate Excel*, there will be some duplication both in terms of the functions covered as well as some of the topics around functions, like how to copy formulas and keep cell references fixed. But I think there is enough new content in this book that you'll still find value in it.

Do you need to read a book about the top fifty functions in Excel to use it effectively? No. You could stop with *Excel for Beginners* and be fine for most day to day uses. But using formulas and functions in Excel will allow you to take your usage of Excel to the next level. And I believe this book is a great introduction to that topic.

As with the other books in the series, this book is written using Excel 2013. Anyone with a version of Excel prior to Excel 2007 is going to be working in a version of Excel that looks very different and may be limited in its list of available functions. For example, SUMIFS and COUNTIFS were not available in versions of Excel prior to Excel 2007.

So that's what this book covers. Let's get started with an overview of how formulas and functions work.

HOW FORMULAS AND FUNCTIONS WORK

If you are writing a basic mathematical formula in Excel you do so by starting your entry in a cell with a plus (+), a minus (-) or an equals (=) sign. Unless you have a good reason for doing so, like years of ingrained habit, I recommend just using the equals sign.

So if I want to add two values together in Excel, I would enter something like this into the cell:

=2+3

I could also do so using cell references if those values were already stored in cells in my worksheet:

=A1+B1

(If you aren't familiar with cell notation in Excel, see Appendix A.)

When I hit Enter or otherwise leave that cell, Excel will display the result of the formula in the cell. In the top example, that means it would display the value 5 in the cell. Excel will, however, retain the formula that was used to calculate that value. You can either double-click in the cell or click on the cell and look to the formula bar to see the formula.

Excel formulas can use basic mathematical notation or they can use functions to perform specified tasks.

To add two numbers together in Excel you use the plus (+) sign between the values like I did above. To subtract one number from another you use the minus (-) sign. To multiply two numbers you use the asterisk (*) sign. To divide two numbers you use the forward slash (/). So:

=3-2 would subtract 2 from 3

=3*2 would multiply 3 times 2

=3/2 would divide 3 by 2

As I mentioned above, your formulas can either use cell references or numbers. So:

=A1-B1 would subtract the value in Cell B1 from the value in Cell A1

=A1*B1 would multiply the value in Cell A1 by the value in Cell B1

=A1/B1 would divide the value in Cell A1 by the value in Cell B1

Excel can handle as complex a formula as you want to throw at it. You can combine in one cell a formula that adds multiple values, divides values, subtracts values, and multiplies values as well as any number of other mathematical tasks or functions.

If you're going to combine calculation steps within one cell, you need to be careful that you properly place your parens so that calculations are performed in the correct order. There is a help document on this titled "Calculation operators and precedence in Excel" that lists the order in which calculations are done by Excel and also lists a number of operators (such as > for greater than) that are useful to know when working with formulas and functions in Excel.

If you're building a really complex formula it's always a good idea to test it as you go to make sure that all of the components are working properly and that the end result is the expected result. So I will build each component separately before combining them all in one cell.

Formulas in Excel go beyond the basic mathematical formula you learned in school. They can handle date-based, text-based, and logic-based calculations as well as mathematical calculations. They do this through the use of Excel functions.

Functions are essentially programmed shortcuts that do specific tasks. For example, the SUM function will add all of the values in a range of cells that you identify. Or the CONCATENATE function will take a set of inputs (usually text) and combine them together in one cell.

There are hundreds of functions in Excel that you can use in your formulas.

To use a function, you start a formula with the equals sign, type in the name of the function, use an opening paren, provide the inputs required for that function, and then use a closing paren.

So to sum a range of cells from A1 through A3, which we'll cover more when we start working through the fifty functions covered by this book, you would type

=SUM(A1:A3)

The equals sign tells Excel this is a formula, the SUM portion tells Excel that we're using the SUM function, the opening paren says we're going to list inputs for that function, the A1:A3 tell Excel which cells to apply the function to, and then the closing paren says that's the end of the function. It doesn't have to be the end of the formula.

(As we'll discuss at the end, you can combine functions within one formula.)

I could have

$$=SUM(A1:A3) + SUM(C1:C3)$$

That's sloppy notation. I could as easily have written =SUM(A1:A3,C1:C3) and had the same result. But the point here is that a formula starts with an equals sign and then you use functions as part of that formula by using their name followed by opening and closing parens and providing the required information for the particular function within the parens.

Don't worry. We're going to walk through lots and lots of examples of this. You'll get it if you don't now.

Just remember to think of a function, whether it handles text or is logical or performs a mathematical function, as part of a formula. In other words, as part of something that is being calculated based upon your inputs.

Garbage in, garbage out. If you give the function the wrong inputs, you will get the wrong results. So if you get an error message (which we'll discuss at the end) when using a function, check that the information you input into your formula is formatted properly and is of the right type. That's usually where things go wrong.

Alright. Next we'll talk about where to find functions in Excel. But remember, you need an equals sign (⁻) to start a formula and then you can use numbers, cell references, operators, or functions to build that formula.

WHERE TO FIND FUNCTIONS

In this guide we're going to cover the fifty Excel functions I thought were most useful for the largest number of people. But there are far, far more functions than that in Excel. And chances are at some point you'll need one I didn't cover here.

In newer versions of Excel, you can go to the Formulas tab to see what Excel functions are available to you. There is a section called Function Library that lists various categories of functions. Mine shows Recently Used, Financial, Logical, Text, Date & Time, Lookup & Reference, Math & Trig, and then there's a dropdown for More Functions that shows the categories Statistical, Engineering, Cube, Information, Compatibility, and Web.

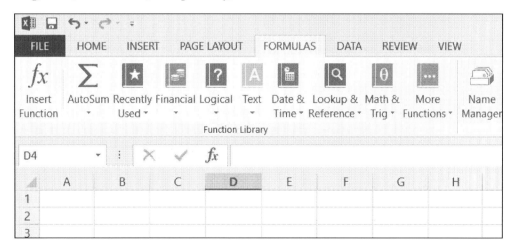

Click on the dropdown arrow next to any of the categories and you'll see a listing of functions that fall under that heading.

Now, unless you know what you're looking for, this listing probably won't help you much because the functions are named things like ACCRINT and IFNA. You can hold your cursor over each of the names and Excel will provide a brief description of the function for you, but for some of the lists that's a lot of functions to look through.

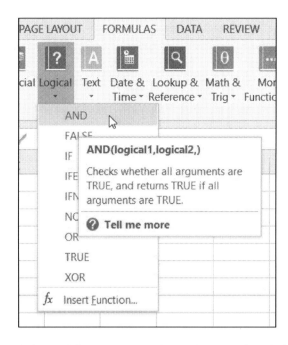

Each description also includes a Tell Me More at the end of the description. If you click on that option, the Excel Help screen will appear. You can then click on "Excel functions (alphabetical)" and choose your desired function from the list. This will show you additional information on the function and how it works.

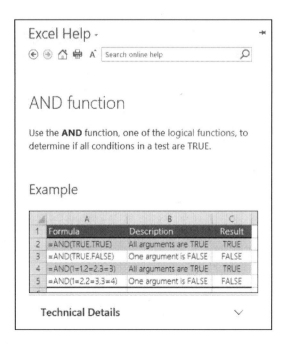

Instead of that, I would recommend that you use the Insert Function option which is also available in the Formulas tab on the far left-hand side.

Be sure you're clicked into an empty cell on your worksheet and then click on Insert Function. This will bring up the Insert Function dialogue box.

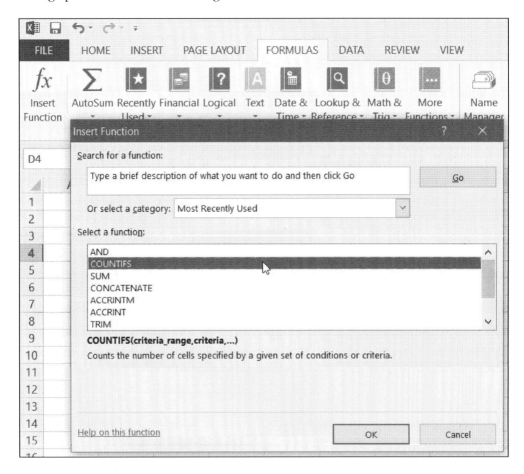

In the top section under where it says "Search for a function" you can type what you're looking to do and then click on Go. (Be sure that the category dropdown right below the search box is set to All unless you know for certain what category your function falls under.)

Excel will provide a list of functions that it thinks meet your search criteria. (Sometimes this list is very far off, so don't just accept the first choice blindly.) You can left-click on each of the listed functions to see a brief description of the function. This appears below the box where the functions are listed.

You will also see for each function a list of the required inputs for that function.

For COUNTIFS you can see in the screenshot above that the first input required is the criteria range and that the second input required is the criteria and that the description of the function is "Counts the number of cells specified by a given set of conditions or criteria."

(In this guide I have listed this information for each function at the top of the function's page.)

If you need more information on a function, you can click on the "Help on this function" link in the bottom left corner of the dialogue box. This will bring up the Excel Help box for that particular function.

Otherwise, you can just click on the function you want and choose OK.

This will insert the function into whichever cell you'd been clicked into before you chose Insert Function. You will also see a Function Arguments dialogue box that lists the inputs your function needs and provides a location for you to input those values.

You can either input numeric values in those boxes or use cell references by clicking on the cells in your worksheet or typing the cell references in.

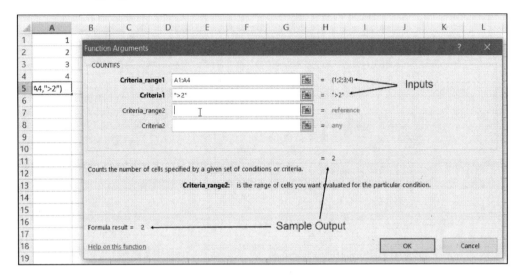

At the bottom of the list of inputs Excel will show you a sample value based upon the inputs you've chosen. The sample also appears in the bottom left corner of the dialogue box.

When you're done, click OK.

* * *

If you already know the function you want to use but aren't sure about the inputs, you can start typing your formula into a cell. After you type equals and the function name you will see a definition for the function.

After you type the opening paren for the function you will see a description of the inputs needed for the function listed directly below the cell.

4	4		
5	=countif(		
6	COUNTIF(**range**, criteria)		
7			

If you click on the function name after you've typed the opening paren, Excel will open the Excel Help dialogue box specific to that function.

* * *

If none of that works to help you find the function you need, then an Internet search is probably your best option.

A quick search for something like "How do I get Excel to identify the day of the week from a date?" will usually get you the answer you need. You can then use the Excel help for that formula either from within Excel or from the Microsoft website to guide you. (Or watch a free video on how to do it.)

* * *

One final note.

In older versions of Excel the Formulas tab didn't exist, so what I would do to bring up that Insert Function dialogue box is I would type equals into a cell and then go to the white dropdown box to the left of the formula bar, click on that dropdown arrow, and choose More Function from the bottom of the list.

This would bring up the Insert Function dialogue box and then I could follow the steps above.

So that's how you find the functions you need, what they do, and what inputs they require.

FORMULA AND FUNCTION BEST PRACTICES

Now let's discuss a few best practices when it comes to using formulas and functions.

Make Your Assumptions Visible

You're going to see as we move forward that you can build a formula that uses a function where all of the information to make the calculation is contained within that one cell.

So if I want to add the values 10, 20, and 30 together I can do that in one cell using the SUM function, =SUM(10,20,30), and all anyone will see in the worksheet is the result of that calculation, 60.

You may be tempted to do this because it's clean. All that people see is what you want them to, the result of your calculation.

And maybe you don't expect to have to adjust those values so you don't see an issue in having your formula built that way.

I would encourage you not to do this. In my experience, a best practice in terms of building formulas is to have any fixed values or assumptions visible in the worksheet. The reason to do this is so that someone looking at the sheet can see what assumptions fed the calculation.

Here's an example:

Let's say you're calculating how much you'll make if you sell your house. You figure you'll have to spend $2,500 to clean the place up a bit, pay a commission of 5%, and that the house is worth $500,000.

Now, if you sat down to discuss this with your spouse you could just show them the results of that calculation (the value on the left) or you could show them the results of the calculation and the assumptions you made (the value on the right).

A	B	C	D	E
	Option 1			Option 2
			Home Price	$500,000.00
Net	$472,500.00		Commission	5%
			Fix Up Cost	$2,500.00
			Net	$472,500.00

Option 2 is more useful, because you can both see what assumptions were made and acknowledge and validate each one. Maybe your spouse knows that houses in the area have been selling for $400,000 instead of $500,000 or that the neighbors up the street worked with a great broker who only charges 4% commission. Without showing them your assumptions, they aren't given a chance to provide their input.

If you bury your assumptions in your calculation field they're easy to forget about. And that can be dangerous if they're wrong.

So I strongly urge you to always have your assumptions present and visible in your worksheet rather than buried in your formulas.

Use Paste Special - Values

The other thing I do that you may or may not want to do depending on why you're using Excel is that I frequently use Paste Special – Values when I'm done with performing a set of calculations.

Do not do this if the calculations you performed need to be updated on an ongoing basis.

But I do a lot of calculations where I want to keep the results for reference but will not be recalculating any values. In this case I want to lock those values down so that I don't lose them or inadvertently recalculate them by changing a value in an input cell or deleting data that fed those calculations.

The simple way to do this is to select the cells, Ctrl + C to copy, and then right-click and under Paste Special choose the Values option (the one with the 123 on the clipboard). This will replace any calculated cells in that range with just the values of the calculation.

After you do that, instead of a formula that says "add Cells A1 and B1 together" you'll have a cell that just contains the result of having added Cells A1 and B1 together. Now if you delete Cells A1 and B1 or change their values, your result field won't change.

Don't Mess With Your Raw Data

I mentioned this in the other books, but am going to mention it again here.

To the extent possible, you should always store your raw data in one location and do all of your calculations and manipulations on that data elsewhere. (Ideally you would also record all of the steps you followed to take that raw data and turn it into your final product, but it's not as easy to do in something like Excel as it is in a program like R.)

If you don't do this, all it takes is one bad sort or one bad function and your data can be irreparably changed if you don't catch it right away.

If you keep your raw data separate there is nothing you can't come back from. You might have to redo a lot of work, but you won't be left with a dataset that's useless.

I also save versions of my worksheets when I'm working on something particularly complicated. That way I can go back to a stage where everything was working without having to start over from scratch. Just be sure to label your files clearly so that you know which is the most recent version. (File V1, File V2, etc.)

Test Your Formulas

If I'm going to apply a formula to a large range of data I will usually test that formula on a much smaller sample of my data where I can visually evaluate the results. So if I'm writing a formula to sum customer transactions for customers from Alaska who bought Widgets (using SUMIFS), I'll run that formula against just ten rows of data to make sure that it's doing what I think it should before I apply it to ten thousand rows of data.

As much as possible you should always either check you formulas on a subset of data or "gut check" your results. Don't just accept the value Excel gives you without questioning whether it actually makes sense. (Because garbage in, garbage out. Excel's ability to perform calculations is limited by your ability to write those calculations properly. And we all make mistakes. One missing $ sign or one > instead of >= and the result you get will not be the result you wanted.)

Test, test, test. And then check, check, check.

COPYING FORMULAS

Before we move into discussing specific functions, I want to cover how to copy formulas and keep cell references fixed.

One of the most powerful aspects of Excel, for me, is in the fact that I can write a formula once, copy it, and paste it to thousands of cells, and it will automatically adjust to its new location

It's fantastic.

When that's what you want.

When copying a formula always check the formula first to be sure that it's going to copy well.

The biggest issue I run into with copying formulas is failing to lock down cells that need to be fixed references.

So if I've put interest rate in Cell A1 and I need every single calculation no matter the row to reference Cell A1, then I need to lock down that cell reference before I copy the formula. You do this by using $ signs in your formula.

To lock an entire cell reference use dollar signs in front of both the column and the row identifier. So $A$1 will always reference the cell in Column A and Row 1 no matter where I copy that formula to.

To lock just the column reference, put a dollar sign in front of the column identifier. So $A1. This will ensure that no matter where the formulas is copied to, that cell will always reference Column A. The row number, however, will be able to adjust. (I use this in my two-variable analysis grid.)

To lock the row reference, put a dollar sign in front of the row identifier. So A$1. This will ensure that no matter where the formula is copied to, the cell will always reference Row 1. The column reference, however, will change.

I find that when I'm copying formulas I need to check for not only fixed values, like the interest rate example above, but also for cell ranges.

For example, if I want to know what percent of my overall sales each product was and I have a list of sales by product I can calculate that by taking the sales for each product divided by the total sales for all products. If I take that total sales by referencing a cell range, such as A1:A25, then before I copy that formula down my row of values I need to lock in that range by writing it as $A$1:$A$25.

If I don't do that, in the next row down that cell range will change to be A2:A26 instead of A1:A25.

So always check before copying.

And if you just need to move a formula to a new location but don't want any of the cell references to adjust then you need to cut and move the formula instead of copying it.

OK. That's it for the preliminaries. Time to start talking about specific functions. We'll start with some basic Math & Trig ones first.

THE SUM FUNCTION

Notation: SUM(number1, [number2],…)
Excel Definition: Adds all the numbers in a range of cells.

The SUM function is probably the most basic function in Excel and I'd suspect the most widely used. What the SUM function does is add numbers together. These can be numbers that you type directly into the function (not recommended as discussed above under best practices) or they can be values that are stored in other cells. Cells do not need to be touching for their values to be added together, although it's much easier to write your SUM function if they are.

To use the function you use SUM and must include at least one number (or cell range) within the parens.

Some examples of formulas that use the SUM function are:

$$=SUM(2,3,4)$$

Adds the numbers 2, 3, and 4 together. So it's the same as using =2+3+4 as your formula.

$$=SUM(A1,A2,A3)$$

This formula does the exact same thing as the first formula except it's using cell references to add the values in Cells A1, A2, and A3 together. You could also type =A1+A2+A3 in a cell and get the same result.

$$=SUM(A1:A3)$$

This is where the SUM function becomes necessary. It's a cleaner way to write the second example since we've replaced A1, A2, A3 with A1:A3. Because of that cell notation it requires use of the SUM function to work.

$$=SUM(A1:A3,B2:B6)$$

This one is saying to add all the values in the range from Cell A1 to Cell A3 (so Cells A1, A2, and A3) as well as all the values in the range from Cell B2 to Cell B6 (so Cells B2, B3, B4, B5, and B6). Because of the use of the cell ranges, this one also requires use of the SUM function. The alternative would be to write =A1+A2+A3+B2+B3+B4+B5+B6 which no one wants to do.

$$=SUM(A:A)$$

This example is saying to sum all of the values in Column A.

$$=SUM(5:5)$$

This example is saying to sum all of the values in Row 5.

* * *

Neither of those last two can be easily replaced with a formula that uses the plus sign. They demonstrate how powerful such a simple function can be.

So, pretty simple, right? An equals sign, SUM, opening paren, whatever you want to add together using cell notation, closing paren. Done.

And as I mentioned above, you can also combine functions in a larger formula. So, for example, if I had a value in Cell A1 and I wanted to subtract all of the values in Column C, I could write that as:

$$=A1-SUM(C:C)$$

Or if I wanted to subtract the values in Column C from A1 but then also add the values in Column E, I could do that as well:

$$=A1-SUM(C:C)+SUM(E:E)$$

Note that when a function doesn't start a formula that you don't need to put the equals sign in front of it.

Alright.

Let's move on to PRODUCT which is another simple one, although I would expect much less popular.

THE PRODUCT FUNCTION

Notation: PRODUCT(number1, [number2],…)
Excel Definition: Multiplies all the numbers given as arguments.

The PRODUCT function does for multiplication what the SUM function does for addition. It will multiply all of the values that you include in the parens by one another.

A few examples:

$$=PRODUCT(2,3,4)$$

Multiplies 2 times 3 times 4.

$$=PRODUCT(A1:A3)$$

Multiplies the value in Cell A1 times the value in Cell A2 times the value in Cell A3.

$$=PRODUCT(A:A)$$

Multiplies all of the values in Column A times one another. So Cell A1 times Cell A2 times Cell A3, etc.

You could also just multiply values times one another using an asterisk (*). The top two examples above could be written as the following:

$$=2*3*4$$

$$=A1*A2*A3$$

But the value of PRODUCT comes in when you have a large range of values that you need to multiply times one another, like the last example which has 65,536 potential values.

Of course there aren't many circumstances where you'll want to multiply that many numbers times one another, which is why I suspect the function is rarely used.

The reason I've included it here is because of the next function we're going to discuss, SUMPRODUCT, which combines summing and multiplying values.

THE SUMPRODUCT FUNCTION

Notation: SUMPRODUCT(array1, [array2], [array3],…)
Excel Definition: Returns the sum of the products of corresponding ranges or arrays.

You use SUMPRODUCT when you have a range of cells that need to be multiplied times one another, like number of units and price to get total cost per product, and then summed, to get total cost, for example.

SUMPRODUCT is incredibly useful when you need it. You could get the same result using a combination of SUM and PRODUCT, but why do that when one little function will do it for you.

Now, that definition and the use of "array" in the Excel notation for the function probably seem a little intimidating. Don't worry, they're not.

Let's walk through an example:

	A	B	C	D	E
1	Product	Units Bought	Price Per Unit	Income	Formulas in Column D
2	Widget	3	$ 2.50	$ 7.50	=B2*C2
3	Whatsit	4	$ 3.20	$12.80	=B3*C3
4	Whatchamacallit	6	$ 4.40	$26.40	=B4*C4
5	Whatnot	2	$ 5.50	$11.00	=B5*C5
6					
7			Total Earned	$57.70	=SUM(D2:D5)
8			Total Earned	$57.70	=SUMPRODUCT(B2:B5,C2:C5)
9					

What we have here is a list of products bought by a customer. We have product name, number of units bought, and price paid per unit.

To calculate the total amount spent you could multiply units times price paid for each product and then sum those values. That's what happens in Cells D2 through D7. In Cells D2 through D5 we have the amount spent on each product (the formulas used are shown in Column E), and then in D7 we have the sum of those values. (That formula is also shown in Column E.)

Your other option is to use the SUMPRODUCT function. That's what happens in Cell D8. The formula, =SUMPRODUCT(B2:B5,C2:C5) is shown in Cell E8.

As you can see above in the Excel notation, SUMPRODUCT requires that you tell it the ranges of the cells that need to be multiplied by one another. In this case, our first range of values was number of units which is in Cells B2 through B5 and our second range of values was price per unit which is in Cells C2 through C5.

What SUMPRODUCT does is it takes the value from the first cell in each provided range, in this case Cells B2 and C2, and multiplies those values. It then does the same with the values in the second cell in each range, in this case the values in Cells B3 and C3. It continues to do this for the entire range. Once it has those multiplied values it then sums them together to get the final result.

It does everything we did in Cells D2 though D7, but in one step. Like I said, very useful when you need it.

A few things to be aware of. The ranges you input into the function need to be the same size for this to work. If they aren't you will get a #VALUE! result instead.

Also, be sure that the ranges you choose have numbers in them and not text. Excel will treat non-numeric values as zeros and any number times zero is…zero.

And, while the example I used above had values in two columns you are not limited to just two columns of values. (Just be sure the cells you select should be multiplied by one another and then added. So I could've had another column in there for sales tax, for example.) And you can also use SUMPRODUCT with values that are in rows instead or in a combination of rows and columns. The key is that the ranges you specify have to be the same dimension, so the same number of columns and rows.

THE AVERAGE FUNCTION

Notation: AVERAGE(number1, [number2],…)
Excel Definition: Returns the average (arithmetic mean) of its arguments, which can be numbers or names, arrays, or references that contain numbers.

The three functions we just discussed are all listed by Excel under the Math & Trig category. This next one, AVERAGE, is listed as a Statistical function, but when I think about taking an average I generally think of it along with addition and division so I'm including it here.

The definition above is slightly confusing when you read it, so let's rewrite it to clarify. Let's write it as this: The AVERAGE function returns the average (arithmetic mean) of its arguments. The arguments can be numbers like 1, 2, 3, or 4. Or the arguments can be a named range, an array, or a cell reference as long as the cells or range referenced include numbers.

What the AVERAGE function does is it takes the sum of a range of numbers and then divides that sum by the number of entries in the range that had a value.

For example, if I have the values 1, 2, 3, 4, and 5 in a range of 5 cells from A1 through A5 and I write =AVERAGE(A1:A5), Excel will add those values to get 15, divide that total by 5, and return a value of 3.

If I include Cell A6, a blank cell, in that range and write it as =AVERAGE(A1:A6), I get the same result even though I now have six cells in my range, because AVERAGE only looks at those cells that have values in them.

This is very important. And may not be what you wanted.

If you have a cell in your range that should be included but where the value is blank instead of zero, you need to put a zero in that cell or it will not be included in your calculation.

In our example above, putting a zero in Cell A6 changes our average to 2.5 from 3 because we're now dividing 15 by 6 instead of 5.

Here's are all three scenarios side-by-side with the formula used shown above each result.

	A	B	C
1	**Value Range**	**Value Range**	**Value Range**
2	1	1	1
3	2	2	2
4	3	3	3
5	4	4	4
6	5	5	5
7			0
8	=AVERAGE(A1:A5)	=AVERAGE(B1:B6)	=AVERAGE(C1:C6)
9	**3**	**3**	**2.5**

AVERAGE will, of course, also work on values that you enter directly in the formula. So =AVERAGE(1,2,3,4,5) would return a value of 3. (But doing this is not recommended, as discussed in the best practices chapter.)

If you use AVERAGE on a range of cells that include text in some of the cells, those cells that contain text will be ignored and treated the same as a blank cell, so not counted for the divisor.

For example, in the sample below even though there are five cells referenced by =AVERAGE(H2:H6) Excel is summing the numeric values in Cells H3 through H5 and dividing them by 3. It ignores Cell H2 which has text and Cell H6 which is blank.

	H
1	**Value Range**
2	Alpha
3	1
4	2
5	3
6	=AVERAGE(H2:H6)
7	2

So if you have a range that you are going to take an average from and you use AVERAGE be sure that the range only contains numbers and that all cells in the range that you want included in your calculation have a zero or a number in them.

THE AVERAGEA FUNCTION

Notation: AVERAGEA(value1, [value2],…)
Excel Definition: Returns the average (arithmetic mean) of its arguments, evaluating text and FALSE in arguments as 0; TRUE evaluates as 1. Arguments can be numbers, names, arrays, or references.

If you need to take an average from a range that has non-numeric values in it and you need those cells included when calculating the average, you can use AVERAGEA to do so.

As it says in the definition, AVERAGEA treats text entries and FALSE values as having a value of 0 and TRUE values as having a value of 1 when calculating the arithmetic mean.

For example, if I have a range of cells and they have the numeric values 10 and 6 and then the text values "This" and "That" in them, like this:

	A	B
1	10	
2	6	
3	This	
4	That	
5	4	=AVERAGEA(A1:A4)
6	8	=AVERAGE(A1:A4)

If I use AVERAGEA to take the average of those four cells, the value it returns is 4 because it takes 10+6 and then divides that by the number of cells with values in it, 4. 16 divided by 4 is 4.

If I use AVERAGE on that same range of cells, the value Excel returns is 8 because it takes 10+6 but then only divides by the number of cells that have numbers in them, 2. 16 divided by 2 is 8.

You will need to decide based on your data which function, AVERAGE or AVERAGEA, is the appropriate choice. With both of them, however, know that a completely blank cell will be skipped over in calculating the average, so you still need a zero value or something in each cell if you want that cell included in the calculation.

As noted in the definition, AVERAGEA also counts TRUE values as 1 when taking an average. So if you want to know the average outcome of a scenario, you could use an IF function to generate TRUE and FALSE values and then use AVERAGEA to calculate the average number of times the outcome occurred.

Here I've done so with a scenario to determine if the entries in Column G were greater than 11. The IF function (which we cover later) returns a value of TRUE if the value is over 11 and FALSE if it is not. I then used AVERAGEA to calculate the average outcome.

	G	H	I
1	2	FALSE	
2	10	FALSE	
3	12	TRUE	
4	14	TRUE	
5		0.5	=AVERAGEA(H1:H4)
6		#DIV/0!	=AVERAGE(H1:H4)
7			

AVERAGEA returns a result of .5 since half of the time the result was TRUE and half of the time the result was FALSE. As you can see, AVERAGE returns an error message, #DIV/0!, because there were no values to include in the average calculation so Excel tried to divide by zero which it can't do.

THE MEDIAN FUNCTION

Notation: MEDIAN(number1, [number2],…)
Excel Definition: Returns the median, or the number in the middle of the set of given numbers.

The average calculation is very useful and very commonly used. But it can sometimes give very misleading results. That's where MEDIAN and MODE come in. They provide a better picture when your data is skewed in some way.

For example, writing income is highly skewed. (As is acting income.) There's someone out there making $100,000 a month and a lot of other someones out there making $10 a month.

If you average those incomes you'll see an average of $10,000 a month, which looks really good. But the reality is that it's either be that one person making $100,000 a month or everyone else making $10 a month. (Not really, but close.)

The average doesn't show this, but the median will.

So if you don't know the nature of your data, it's always a good idea to take both the average and the median and compare them.

If the data is evenly distributed (spread out nicely) then they'll give you similar results. But if it's skewed, like in my example above, you'll have vastly different outcomes.

To get the median, just give Excel your range.

In the example below I've used

=MEDIAN(A1:A9)

to calculate the median of the values in Cells A1 through A9:

◢	A	B
1	1	
2	1	
3	1	
4	1	
5	1	
6	1	
7	1	
8	1	
9	100	
10	1	=MEDIAN(A1:A9)
11	12	=AVERAGE(A1:A9)

It's that simple. (And, as you can see, because of the 100 value in that range compared to the 1s in all the other cells, MEDIAN and AVERAGE return very different results.)

If you give Excel a range that has an even number of values, so there isn't just one middle value, Excel will average the two middle values and return their average. So =MEDIAN(1,2,3,4) will return 2.5 which is the average of the middle two values, 2 and 3.

(Be careful with this. Because =MEDIAN(1,100) would return a value of 50.5 which is very misleading. In general, it's a good idea to chart or visually inspect a dataset so you can see when situations like this exist.)

Median also works on logical values (TRUE, FALSE) that are typed directly into the argument. So

=MEDIAN(TRUE,TRUE,FALSE)

will return a value of 1 and

=MEDIAN(FALSE,FALSE,TRUE)

will return a value of 0.

But if you reference a range with TRUEs and FALSEs in it you'll get a #NUM! error.

I'm not sure how much good it does you that you can type it into the function directly, but that's the way it works. If you do ever have a set of TRUE/FALSE results, you can always convert them to ones and zeros using an IF function and then take the median of the ones and zeros.

THE MODE FUNCTION

Notation: MODE(number1, [number2],…)
Excel Definition: Returns the most frequently occurring, or repetitive, value in an array or range of data.

Excel has a note on the MODE function that it only exists for compatibility with Excel 2007 or earlier. For those of you using Excel 2013 or later, you should look to MODE.SNGL and MODE.MULT instead.

MODE goes along with AVERAGE and MEDIAN as a possible way to look at your data and to figure out the result that most people will see.

As we discussed above, AVERAGE doesn't work well if your data has a high skew to it. So if most people score really low and there are just a few people who score really high then looking at an average is going to mislead you about how the average person will do. MEDIAN can sometimes be a better measure because it looks at the result in the exact middle.

But MEDIAN also has a flaw. And that's that it's not very good with data that has spikes that aren't near the median. Look at the following example:

	A	B	C	D	E
1	1				
2	1				
3	3				
4	3				
5	4		AVERAGE	94.67	=AVERAGE(A1:A12)
6	4		MEDIAN	17.00	=MEDIAN(A1:A12)
7	30		MODE	30.00	=MODE(A1:A12)
8	30				
9	30				
10	30				
11	500				
12	500				

There are twelve values to analyze. I've taken those values and used the COUNTIF function to figure out how many times each value occurs. You can see that 1, 3, 4, and 500 each occur two times and that 30 occurs four times.

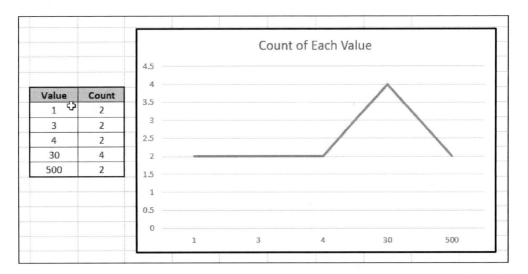

So if you were placing a bet on which number was most likely to occur, you'd want to bet on the 30. Right? If you had to choose just one of the five values, 30 would be the most likely outcome.

But the average of these numbers is approximately 95 and the median is 17. (The median is 17 because since there are an even number of values Excel takes the two closest to the center, in this case a 4 and a 30, and averages them.)

Neither of those functions comes close to providing the right answer.

But MODE, which returns the most frequently occurring outcome, will return a value of 30.

What it does is basically build a count table like I just did and then return the outcome with the highest number of occurrences.

Because in this case the most common outcome is not around the center, looking for the mode is the only way to predict the most likely outcome with any sort of accuracy.

(This is also why if you're dealing with a dataset that you're not familiar with it's good to visualize the data. The spike at 30 is very clear when we plot the count of each value. If you don't have discrete values, you can put a range of values in groups and plot the count of how many values fall in each group instead.)

MODE works just like AVERAGE and MEDIAN. Just give it a range of cells to evaluate:

$$=MODE(A1:A12)$$

In Excel 2013 and later versions of Excel the basic MODE function has been replaced with two new functions, MODE.SNGL and MODE.MULT, so let's talk about those next.

THE MODE.SNGL FUNCTION

Notation: MODE.SNGL(number1, [number2],…)
Excel Definition: Returns the most frequently occurring, or repetitive, value in an array or range of data.

MODE.SNGL is the exact same as MODE. See above for how that works. The big change that occurred with Excel 2013 was the introduction of MODE.MULT. So let's talk about that next.

THE MODE.MULT FUNCTION

Notation: MODE.MULT(number1, [number2],…)
Excel Definition: Returns a vertical array of the most frequently occurring, or repetitive, values in an array or range of data.

The MODE.MULT function allows you to have Excel return more than one value when it calculates the mode for a range of values. So if you have multi-modal data (meaning there are multiple bumps in your data), using MODE.MULT will return those multiple values.

Now, there's a trick to using it.

And that's that it's considered an array formula. (Yeah, I'd never heard of it before either. There's a reason I've never written a book called *Advanced Excel*. But we'll cover it here in this one limited example so that we've fully discussed calculating the mode of a range of numbers.)

To use MODE.MULT you need a range of values that you're going to use for your mode calculation and a range of cells where you're going to put the result of that calculation.

Highlight the range of cells where you want your *results* to be displayed. You need to highlight enough cells to allow Excel to provide all possible values. (This is why plotting your data is a good idea. If you've plotted your data and seen that it has two equal-sized bumps in it, then you would know to highlight two cells. Otherwise you can guess and Excel will just return an #N/A value for the cells it doesn't use.)

In the example below, I highlighted Cells D5 through D8.

Once you have your cells highlighted where you want your results to display, *then* you type your formula into the formula bar.

In the example below I typed:

=MODE.MULT(A1:A10)

Then, and this is crucial because it won't work otherwise, instead of typing Enter, you need to type Ctrl + Shift + Enter all at the same time.

You'll know you've done it right, because when you click back into the cell the formula will have little brackets around it. Like this:

$$\{=MODE.MULT(A1:A10)\}$$

That exact same formula will appear in all of the cells you highlighted, not just the top one. And it will calculate the multiple modes in your data. Like this:

	A	B	C	D	E
1	1				
2	3		AVERAGE	63.3	=AVERAGE(A1:A10)
3	3		MEDIAN	16.5	=MEDIAN(A1:A10)
4	3		MODE	3	=MODE(A1:A10)
5	3			3	{=MODE.MULT(A1:A10)}
6	30		MODE.MULT	30	{=MODE.MULT(A1:A10)}
7	30			#N/A	{=MODE.MULT(A1:A10)}
8	30			#N/A	{=MODE.MULT(A1:A10)}
9	30				
10	500				
11					

Here we have a dataset where 1 and 500 occur once and 3 and 30 occur four times. When I plot this data you can see that it's multi-modal, meaning it has more than one peak value. The likely outcome is either 3 or 30.

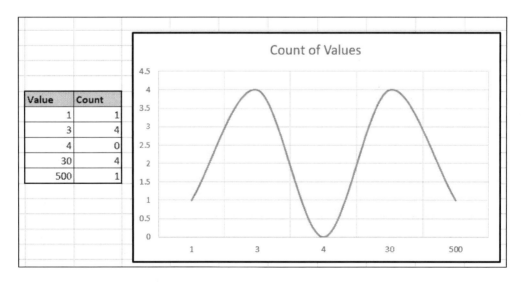

If I take just the average of these values, though, I get 63.3. And if I take the median I get 16.5. And if I take the basic mode which existed in earlier versions of Excel I get 3, because it returns the first most frequent value in my data.

But with MODE.MULT, Excel returns both 3 and 30.

Isn't that great?

And if you wanted your results to display in a single row instead of a single column, you just write the formula as =TRANSPOSE(MODE.MULT(A1:A10)) instead.

Very useful. But also only available in Excel 2013 or later.

(But you still need to be careful when you use this. It's not perfect. Because it only returns the most frequently occurring value(s). So if one value occurs 12 times and another occurs 11 it will only return the one that occurs 12 times. But it's better than nothing.)

THE MIN FUNCTION

Notation: MIN(number1, [number2],…)
Excel Definition: Returns the smallest number in a set of values. Ignores logical values and text.

Another useful Statistical function is the MIN function. This one takes a range of values or list of numbers and returns the smallest value.

You could say =MIN(1,2,3) and it would return a value of 1 or =MIN(-1,0,1) and it would return a value of -1, but the real power of this function is when you use it on a range of cells.

So, for example, let's say you want to know the lowest test score from a class that had 125 students in it and where all of the test scores were recorded in Column C. You would simply write the function as =MIN(C:C) and it would return for you the lowest test score in the range.

According to Excel, if you reference a range and ask Excel to return the minimum value and there are no numbers in the range it will return a value of zero.

Also, if the range contains an error value such as #DIV/0! the function will return that error value. In this case, #DIV/0!.

THE MINA FUNCTION

Notation: MINA(value1, [value2],…)

Excel Definition: Returns the smallest value in a set of values. Does not ignore logical values and text.

MINA is much like MIN except that it *will* consider logical values and text in determining the minimum value.

If you have a range that has TRUE and FALSE values in it, TRUE will be treated as a 1 and FALSE will be treated as a zero. Basic text entries such as "try" are also treated as zeros.

If there are no values in the range, the result will be a zero.

MINA on a range of numbers works just like MIN. So =MIN(1,2,3) and =MINA(1,2,3) both return the value of 1.

On a range that includes text entries and positive numbers only, since MINA treats those text entries as zeros, your result will be a zero. So =MINA(A1:A3) where the value of A1 is "test", the value of A2 is 1, and the value of A3 is 2 will return a value of 0. If there's a negative number included, MINA will return that negative number.

The only place I can see MINA adding value is for data that includes TRUE and FALSE entries.

THE MAX FUNCTION

Notation: MAX(number1, [number2],…)
Excel Definition: Returns the largest value in a set of values. Ignores logical values and text.

MAX is the counterpart to MIN. Where MIN looks for the smallest value in the range, MAX looks for the largest value in the range.

So =MAX(1,2,3) will return a value of 3 because that's the largest number in the list of provided values. Once again, though, the optimal use of MAX is by applying it to a cell range, such as an entire column or row.

=MAX(4:4) would return the maximum value in Row 4 of your worksheet.

If there are no numbers in the specified range MAX will return a value of 0.

If there is a cell that has an error message within the range, MAX will return that error message.

MAX ignores text entries and does not include logical values like TRUE or FALSE in its determination.

You could use the MAX function to find the largest transaction in a series of transactions or the highest test score, for example.

THE MAXA FUNCTION

Notation: MAXA(value1, [value2],…)
Excel Definition: Returns the largest value in a set of values. Does not ignore logical values and text.

MAXA is much like MINA except it calculates a maximum value instead of a minimum value. And, just as MINA did compared to MIN, MAXA incorporates logical values into its determination.

So if you have a range that has TRUE and FALSE values in it, those will be considered. TRUE will be treated as a 1 and FALSE will be treated as a 0. Also, text entries are treated as zeros.

As with MINA I think the use of MAXA is very limited. The only place I can see it adding value is if you have TRUE and FALSE in your range of cells and need those incorporated into your calculation. (The reason I've included both functions here is for thoroughness since we covered AVERAGEA and will be covering COUNTA later.)

THE ROUND FUNCTION

Notation: ROUND(number, num_digits)
Excel Definition: Rounds a number to a specified number of digits.

ROUND is a simple but potentially useful function. It takes a value and rounds that value to a specified number of digits.

(You can use the formatting options in Excel to give the appearance of having rounded a number. So Number or Currency or Accounting will all format a number to show two decimal places, but using the ROUND function actually transforms the number so that it now only has that number of decimal places.)

The inputs into the ROUND function are the value you want to round and then the number of digits to round that number to.

If you use 0 for num_digits, the number will be rounded to the nearest integer. So =ROUND(111.2345,0) will return 111 as the value.

If you use a number, such as 2, for num_digits the number will be rounded to that many decimal places. So =ROUND(111.2345,2) will return 111.23 as the value.

If you use a negative number for num_digits, such as -2, the number will be rounded to that number of 10's, 100's, 1000's places, etc.

So =ROUND(111.2345,-2) will return 100 as the value.

ROUND will not force a specific number of decimal places on a number, however. For example, if I use =ROUND(1.23,4) which means to round the number 1.23 to the fourth decimal place, ROUND will return a value of 1.23 not 1.2300. (You would need to use TEXT to enforce that type of formatting or you would need to format your cells that way using one of the number formatting options.)

The way Excel decides whether to round up or round down is by looking at the digit one past the one you're going to keep. If that digit is a 0 through a 4, Excel will round down. (Thus keeping the rest of the number unchanged.) If that digit is a 5 through a 9, Excel will round up and the final digit that you're keeping will go up by one.

This is easier to understand if we look at some examples:

=ROUND(1.234,2) says to change the number 1.234 to a number with just two decimal places. So the question is does that become 1.23 or 1.24? The answer is 1.23 because the digit one past the 3, which is the last digit we're keeping, is a 4. Since that value is in the lower range, 0 through 4, we round down.

=ROUND(1.235,2) says the same thing and we have the same two choices, 1.23 or 1.24. But now our last digit after the one we're keeping is a 5 so we round up and our final value becomes 1.24.

Where it gets interesting, for me, is when you have multiple numbers that you're not keeping. So =ROUND(1.2347,2) says to convert 1.2347 to a number with two decimal places as well. If you started at the end and rounded each number at a time you would go from 1.2347 to 1.235 to 1.24. But that's not how Excel works. (And not how rounding in general works either. I looked it up.)

As I explained above, Excel takes the 1.23 that we want to keep and ONLY looks at the next digit in the number. In this case that's a 4 so Excel would round down and return a value of 1.23.

So there you have it. That's how ROUND works. Now on to the two variations on ROUND, ROUNDUP and ROUNDDOWN.

THE ROUNDUP FUNCTION

Notation: ROUNDUP(number, num_digits)
Excel Definition: Rounds a number up, away from zero.

ROUNDUP works much like ROUND except that all numbers are rounded in one direction rather than being split between rounding up and rounding down. In the case of ROUNDUP, all numbers round away from zero. For example,

=ROUNDUP(12.31,1)

and

=ROUNDUP(12.37,1)

will both return a value of 12.4, because that is the value that is away from zero when choosing between 12.3 and 12.4.

If you use ROUNDUP with negative numbers you get the same result except as a negative value. So

=ROUNDUP(-12.31,1)

and

=ROUNDUP(-12.37,1)

both return -12.4 because you still round away from zero.

Be careful when using ROUNDUP (or its counterpart ROUNDDOWN), because there's bias when you only round in one direction. The reason people usually round half of the values up and half of them down is to balance things out over time. If you round up by 2 cents and then down by 3 cents and then up by 4 cents, etc. eventually you come pretty close to zero when you add all the amounts you shaved off together.

But ROUNDUP and ROUNDDOWN can have a purpose.

For example, when I'm estimating numbers for my budget I like to always round what I owe upward and what I'm going to get paid downward. This means I always err in my favor because I always think I have to pay more than I do and that I'm going to earn less than I am. By doing this I guarantee that actual results will always be better than I'd expected. (In college this trick was the only reason I had $40 to pay for groceries at the end of some months...)

So this can have its uses. But generally you'll want to stick with using the ROUND function instead. (Especially if you're a company collecting something like sales tax and don't want to get sued for taking people's money. Those fractions of pennies add up.)

THE ROUNDDOWN FUNCTION

Notation: ROUNDDOWN(number, num_digits)
Excel Definition: Rounds a number down, towards zero.

ROUNDDOWN is the counterpart to ROUNDUP. Where ROUNDUP rounds away from zero, ROUNDDOWN will always round towards zero. So, for example,

=ROUNDOWN(12.31,1)

and

=ROUNDDOWN(12.37,1)

will both round to 12.3 because that is the number closest to zero between the two available choices of 12.3 and 12.4.

And the negatives of those examples,

=ROUNDDOWN(-12.31,1)

and

=ROUNDDOWN(-12.37,1)

will both round to -12.3.

As with ROUNDUP, using ROUNDDOWN can introduce bias into your numbers because when you always round in one direction you tend to skew your numbers. But there are times when that can be to your advantage.

Just be sure if you're using either ROUNDUP or ROUNDDOWN that you know why you're doing it and that it makes sense for you to do so in that circumstance. (And that it won't lead you to doing something illegal or fraudulent.)

Your default should be to use ROUND unless you have a good reason not to.

THE COUNT FUNCTION

Notation: COUNT(value1, [value2],…)
Excel Definition: Counts the number of cells in a range that contain numbers.

The COUNT function is a very basic function. Its derivatives, COUNTIF and COUNTIFS are much more useful and we'll discuss those in a moment, but I wanted to first cover COUNT and its extension, COUNTA, which we'll cover in the next section.

What COUNT does is it allows you to count how many cells within your specified range contain a number or a date.

So a range of cells that contain the values 1, 12/31/10, and "one" will be counted as 2 because the first two entries (1 and 12/13/10) are considered numbers, but the last entry ("one") is not. If you have a cell that shows a numeric value due to a formula, so the cell contents are actually =SUM(2,3) but the cell displays 5, that will be counted as well.

Excel says that it will also count an entry such as "1" as a number, but when I tried that it didn't work. So if you're going to use this function on a range, I would test it to make sure that it's counting your numeric entries properly.

Also, a cell can only contain a number or date. For example, "1 day" would not be counted since it includes the number 1 but also the text "day".

The COUNT function itself is very simple to use. For example, =COUNT(A1:A5) will count the number of cells in the range from Cell A1 through Cell A5 that contain a number or date.

You could also write a function such as =COUNT(1,2,3) and it would count the number of numbers or dates in the list within the parens. In this case, three.

If you don't want to limit your count to just numbers and dates, then you need to use COUNTA.

THE COUNTA FUNCTION

Notation: COUNTA(value1, [value2],…)
Excel Definition: Counts the number of cells in a range that are not empty

The COUNTA function allows you to count how many cells within your specified range are not empty. So not just those that contain dates and numbers, but those that contain anything.

So, for example, COUNTA will count the cell that has "1 day" in it as well as the cell that has a date or a number or the text "one". Anything in a cell will result in that cell being counted.

Be careful, however, because it will also count any cell that has a function in it even if that function is not currently displaying a value. (And using copy and then paste special – values to replace that function may not clear the cell enough for COUNTA to ignore it. You have to make sure that a cell is truly blank for it to not be counted.)

Once again, if you're going to use this test it on a small range to make sure that it works as expected.

To write a COUNTA function just include the cell range(s) you want to count within the parens. So =COUNTA(A1:B30) will count how many cells between Cell A1 and Cell B30 are not empty.

THE COUNTBLANK FUNCTION

Notation: COUNTBLANK(range)
Excel Definition: Counts the number of empty cells in a specified range of cells.

Since we covered COUNTA which counts the number of cells in a range that have are not empty, we might as well cover its counterpart, COUNTBLANK, which counts the number of cells that are empty.

According to Excel, formulas that return empty text ("") are counted as blank, but cells with zero values are not. I tested this with an IF function that returned a value of "", a value of " ", and a value of 0. The one that returned a value of "" was counted as blank, the other two were not.

This is important to know because a cell with a formula that returns a value of "" and one with a formula that returns a value of " " will look the same, but they perform differently when functions like this one are applied to them.

As always, be sure to check a sample of your data to see that the result you are getting is the result you expect and want. If it isn't, with COUNTBLANK you should look to the nature of your data.

THE COUNTIF FUNCTION

Notation: COUNTIF(range, criteria)
Excel Definition: Counts the number of cells within a range that meet the given condition.

For users of Excel 2007 or later, you can use the COUNTIFS function as a substitute for the COUNTIF function.

COUNTIF looks at a range of cells and it counts whether or not the specified condition is met. The first information you provide for the function is the range of cells you want evaluated. Then you specify what criteria must be met.

The criteria can be a cell reference, text, or numeric.

For example:

=COUNTIF(A1:A5,B2) says to count how many times the values in Cells A1 through A5 are the same as the value in Cell B2.

=COUNTIF(A1:A5,"YES") says to count how many times the values in Cells A1 through A5 are the text YES. It will only count those instances where the full value in the cell matches the value given in the quotes. So a cell that says YES, PLEASE would not be counted. Or one that has YES followed by an extra space would not be counted. It has to be an exact match.

=COUNTIF(A1:A5,">20") says to count how many cells between Cell A1 and Cell A5 have a numeric value greater than 20. Note that even though the criteria is related to a number value that it's still shown in quotes because it's an expression. (If you had =COUNTIF(A1:A5,20), which looks for any cells with a value equal to 20, you wouldn't need the quotes but you could still use them.)

If you want to reference a cell for your criteria but you also want to use a greater than or less than symbol, you need to combine the two using an ampersand (&).

For example =COUNTIF(A1:A5,">="&G2) would count how many times the cells in the range from Cell A1 to Cell A5 contain a value that is greater than or equal to the value in Cell G2.

You can also use wildcards with the COUNTIF function if your condition relates to a text value.

The asterisk (*) can be used to count any cell that contains text. You would write that as =COUNTIF(A1:A5,"*").

It can also be used in combination with other letters to, for example, count any entry where there is an e. You would write that as =COUNTIF(A1:A5,"*e*"). The asterisk on either side of the e says to look for any cells where there is an e anywhere.

If you want to count entries of a certain text length you can use the question mark (?) as a wildcard. It represents one single character. So =COUNTIF(A1:A5,"???") would count all cells in the range from Cell A1 through A5 where the entry is three letters or spaces long. (It doesn't work with numbers.)

You can also combine COUNTIF functions if you want to count two criteria within a range. So you can have =COUNTIF(A1:A5,"YES") + COUNTIF(A1:A5,"MAYBE") to count how many cells within the range contained either the value YES or the value MAYBE.

But be careful with this.

If you use something like this: =COUNTIF(A1:A5,"*a*") + COUNTIF(A1:A5,"*e*") where you're counting all entries in the range that contain an a and all entries in the range that contain an e, you can end up double counting.

And if you actually need to find an asterisk or question mark you can do so by using the tilde (~) before the mark you need. So ~? or ~* will look for an actual question mark or an actual asterisk Always test different scenarios to make sure the count is counting everything you want it to but also not more than you want it to. (And be sure you've covered all possible scenarios in your testing, a mistake I know I've made at least once.)

THE COUNTIFS FUNCTION

Notation: COUNTIFS(criteria_range1, criteria1, [criteria_range2, criteria2],...)
Excel Definition: Counts the number of cells specified by a given set of conditions or criteria.

The COUNTIFS function takes the COUNTIF function to the next level by allowing you to specify multiple ranges and multiple criteria that must be met within each of those ranges for an entry to be counted. It is available to users of Excel 2007 or later.

So where COUNTIF would have allowed you to count all customers located in Alabama, for example, COUNTIFS allows you to count all customers located in Alabama, who spent more than $500, and did so in the last six months.

COUNTIFS can substitute for the COUNTIF function. Simply provide only one criteria range and one criteria. (Which means the only difference between the two when the range is a singular range is the use of the S at the end of COUNTIFS.)

To count based upon multiple criteria, simply include additional ranges and criteria for each of those ranges in the function.

The criteria range for all of your criteria must be the same size. So if your first cell range is A1:B25, then your other cell ranges must also be two columns wide and 25 rows long.

Ranges do not have to be adjacent, but they do have to be the same size.

Your criteria, just like with COUNTIF, can be a cell reference (B2), a number (25 or "25"), an expression (">25"), or a text value ("TRUE").

The way the count is performed is it looks at all first cells in each of the criteria ranges and sees if the criteria for each of those ranges are met. If so, that entry is counted. If not, it isn't. It then moves on to the second cell in each of the criteria ranges and checks to see if all of the second cells meet the specified criteria. And so on and so on.

Each time all of the criteria are met, Excel counts that as 1.

Let's walk through an example to see this in action.

Here is a table of six customer transactions that includes the state the customer is from and the total amount they spent.

If we want to know how many customers are from Alabama (AL) who spent $250 or more, we can write a COUNTIFS function to calculate this.

	A	B	C	D
1	**State**	**Total Purchases**		**Customers From AL Who Spent At Least $250**
2	AL	$ 250.00		2
3	AL	$ 125.00		**Cell D2: =COUNTIFS(A2:A7,"AL",B2:B7,">=250")**
4	AZ	$ 110.00		
5	AK	$ 95.00		
6	AR	$ 250.00		
7	AL	$ 300.00		

The function we need is

$$=COUNTIFS(A2:A7,"AL",B2:B7,">=250")$$

And the answer is 2.

Let's break that down.

The first criteria range is A2 through A7. Those are the entries with our State values in them. And we tell Excel we want to count any entry where the state is "AL". That's the first half of our COUNTIFS function.

The second criteria range is B2 through B7. That's our Total Purchases. And we tell Excel that we want to count any time when a value in that range is greater than or equal to $250. That's written as ">=250".

Excel takes the function =COUNTIFS(A2:A7,"AL",B2:B7,">=250") and it starts with Cells A2 and B2 and it says are both criteria met? In this case, yes, so that's counted. Then it moves to A3 and B3 and does the same thing. And on and on through to A7 and B7.

Now if you look at the data, there are three entries where the state is AL and three entries where the customer spent $250 or more. But Excel only counts those entries where both criteria are met. That occurs in Rows 2 and 7.

The entry in Row 3 is for a customer from AL who only spent $125. And the entry in Row 6 is for a customer who did spend $250 but is from AR.

For it to work, when you write a COUNTIFS function you need to make sure that your cell ranges are properly lined up.

And, as you can see above, you can use a different type of criteria for each criteria range. So here I had a text criteria for the first range ("AL") and an expression for the second range (">=250").

Also, as with COUNTIF, you can also use the wildcard symbols for text. So the asterisk (*) and the question mark (?) both work. The asterisk (*) represents any sequence of characters, the question mark (?) represents one single character. And if you want to search for either mark rather than using it as a wildcard, be sure to put a tilde(~) in front of it.

Now on to SUMIF and SUMIFS.

THE SUMIF FUNCTION

Notation: SUMIF(range, criteria, [sum_range])
Excel Definition: Adds the cells specified by a given condition or criteria.

For users of Excel 2007 or later, you can use SUMIFS instead of SUMIF, but be careful of the order of your arguments because they are different.

SUMIF allows you to tell Excel to only sum the values within a range of cells when they meet a specific criteria. For example, you can tell Excel to only sum the values in Cells A1 through A5 that are greater than zero using =SUMIF(A1:A5,">0")

That all occurs within one range of cells. Excel evaluates each cell and only includes the values that meet your specific criteria.

What's more powerful, in my opinion, is that you can use one range to specify your criteria and another to specify the values to sum. For example, using the below data, let's say I wanted to sum the total value of customer transactions (in Column B) that are related to customers from Alabama (in Column A).

	A	B	C	D
1	State	Total Purchases		Sum Orders For Customers From AL
2	AL	$ 250.00		$675.00
3	AL	$ 125.00		Cell D2: =SUMIF(A2:A7,"AL",B2:B7)
4	AZ	$ 110.00		
5	AK	$ 95.00		
6	AR	$ 250.00		
7	AL	$ 300.00		

I could do this with the following formula: =SUMIF(A2:A7,"AL",B2:B7)

The first value, A2:A7, is the range of values that contain my criteria, in this case the state the customer lives in. The next value, "AL", is the criteria that must be met for Excel to include the value in the next range in its calculation. The final value is the sum range, B2:B7. This is where the values I want to add together are stored.

As with COUNTIF and COUNTIFS, you can use criteria that are numeric (23 or "23"), expressions (">25"), or text-based ("AL"). You can also reference a cell (A1) as the criteria.

So you could have =SUMIF(A2:A7,G2,B2:B7) where the value in Cell G2 is what must match the values in Column A in order to sum the values in Column B.

And note that you must use quotation marks around the criteria except for when cell references (G2) or single numbers (23) are involved. (With a single number you can write it with or without the quotes.)

If the criteria used is a text-based criteria, you can also use the wildcards just like you could with COUNTIF and COUNTIFS. So an asterisk (*) stands for any number of characters and a question mark (?) stands for a single character. Because of this, if you're looking to use a criteria that references an actual asterisk or question mark, you need to include a tilde (~) before the mark. So ~* will look for an asterisk, but just * will look for any number of characters.

For example, if I wanted to sum the values in Cells A1 through A6 every time one of the entries in Cells C1 through C6 included a question mark at the end, I could write:

=SUMIF(C1:C6,"*~?",A1:A6)

The asterisk means any text, the tilde means the actual symbol that follows next, and then the question mark there is an actual question mark that we're searching for because of the tilde before it. And, of course, since it's a text-based search term the entirety is surrounded by quotation marks.

Also, you should know that if the match string is too long—in this case 255 or more characters—that SUMIF will return incorrect results.

SUMIF also has a weird quirk in that the sum range does not have to be the same dimensions as the criteria range. Excel will extend the sum range to the size needed if you don't specify the full range or a correctly-sized range.

So, for example, if your criteria range is A1:B25 but you just list C1:C3 as your sum_range Excel will use C1:D25 for its sum_range. It takes the first cell in the range you provide and creates its own range from that.

(I wouldn't rely on this, though. And it doesn't work with SUMIFS so it's a bad habit to get into to let Excel set your sum range for you.)

Alright. That's SUMIF. Those of you with later versions of Excel have a much more powerful option available to you: SUMIFS. Let's discuss that next.

THE SUMIFS FUNCTION

Notation: SUMIFS(sum_range, criteria_range1, criteria1, [criteria_range2, criteria2],…)
Excel Definition: Adds the cells specified by a given set of conditions or criteria.

SUMIFS allows you to sum the values in a range when multiple criteria are met. It can also work just like SUMIF if you only provide one criteria and one criteria range. But be careful, because the inputs into the SUMIFS function are provided in a different order than they're provided for the SUMIF function.

Which is why for those who have access to both (users of Excel 2007 or later) it's probably a good idea to get into the habit of using SUMIFS for everything.

Also, unlike with SUMIF, when using SUMIFS your sum range and the criteria ranges you use need to be the same size. They do not need to be next to one other, but they do need to cover the same number of rows and columns.

Like SUMIF, SUMIFS can use a number (22 or "22"), an expression ("<13"), a text-based criteria ("YES"), or a cell reference (H1) for the sum criteria. For anything except a single number or a cell reference, be sure to use quotation marks around your criteria.

With SUMIFS, just like with COUNTIFS, you don't have to use the same type of criteria for each range. So you can have an expression for one criteria, a cell reference for another, and a text-based criteria for a third.

So I could have

$$=SUMIFS(A1:A25,B1:B25,"USD",C1:C25,">10")$$

That would sum the values in Cells A1 through A25 if the value in the corresponding cells in Cells B1 through B25 contain "USD" and the values in Cells C1 through C25 are greater than 10.

For text-based criteria, you can use the wildcards. So the asterisk (*) to represent any number of characters, the question mark (?) to represent a single character, and the tilde(~) to distinguish when you're actually searching for an asterisk or question mark.

You can have up to 127 criteria. (Why you would want to do that, I don't know. But you can.)

SUMIFS is one of the functions that I use the most.

I use it in my budget worksheet to sum the amount I still owe on my bills each month. So I'll list all of my bills due for the month, whether I pay them with cash or with a credit card (when I was living overseas I would list which currency the bill had to be paid in since I had bills due in both USD and NZD), the amount due, and in a third column I'll put an X when the bill is paid.

The SUMIFS formula I use is =SUMIFS(C1:C10,B1:B10,"CASH",D1:D10,""). So that says sum the values in Column C if the values in Column B are "CASH" and Column D is blank. That lets me know how much cash I need in my bank account before those bills hit.

The other place I use this is with my payables from self-publishing. I am usually owed money at any given time in about five different currencies and from about ten different sources. I have a worksheet where I sum the amount owed in each currency that I haven't yet been paid using a formula similar to the one above. In this case: =SUMIFS(B$3:B$91,D$3:D$91,"USD",E$3:E$91,"")

This says to sum the values in Cells B3 through B91 if the values in Cells D3 through D91 are USD and the values in those cells in Column E are blank. I have a formula like this for each of the currencies I'm owed money in (CAD, AUD, INR, EUR, GBP, etc.) which is what the $ signs help with. This way I can just copy the formula to however many rows I need and all I have to update is the currency abbreviation.

That's just two examples of the power of SUMIFS. If you start to think about it, there are any number of places you can use it. (For me it would be worth upgrading to a current version of Excel if I didn't have it already. You can use multiple SUMIF functions to get the same result, but it's very messy.)

THE AVERAGEIF FUNCTION

Notation: AVERAGEIF(range, criteria, [average_range])
Excel Definition: Finds average (arithmetic mean) for the cells specified by a given condition or criteria.

If you have Excel 2007 or later, AVERAGEIFS can be used in place of AVERAGEIF.

The AVERAGEIF function works just like COUNTIF and SUMIF except it takes an *average* of the values when a specified criteria is met.

An example of when you might use this is if you wanted to know the average customer order amount for customers in different states.

So you could write =AVERAGEIF(F1:F11,"CO",G1:G11) to take the average of the values in Cells G1 through G11 but only when the value in Cells F1 through F11 are CO.

Your criteria can be a cell reference instead which is where this can be really powerful. So in the example above I could've used A1 as the cell reference and had CO in Cell A1 and then all the other states in subsequent cells in Column A.

To calculate the average for all of the states I'd just need to change my cell references to reference the entire column, or if that wasn't possible use $ signs to lock my cell references, and then copy that formula down the number of cells I needed.

The first entry would look like this:

=AVERAGEIF(F:F,A1,G:G)

Or if referencing the columns wasn't possible, it would look like this:

=AVERAGEIF($F$1:$F$11,A1,$G$1:$G$11)

When either of those formulas is copied down the A1 cell reference will change but the other values will not. Meaning I can write that formula once and have it do fifty separate calculations for me just by copying the formula and using a column with all of the states listed.

With AVERAGEIF you can also just average a range of numbers that meet certain criteria without referencing any other column of data.

So if I want to average all values in a column that are over 10, I could say =AVERAGEIF(F:F,">10") and Excel would average the values of all entries in Column F that have a value over 10 and ignore the rest.

Other things to know:

If you have a cell in the range portion that has a value of TRUE or FALSE, Excel will ignore it.

If you have a cell in the average_range portion that is empty, Excel will ignore it.

If a cell in the criteria portion is empty, Excel will treat it as a zero.

If Excel returns a #DIV/0! error, that likely means that there was nothing for it to average, which means the criteria you set weren't met or the range you provided is a blank or text value.

And as with COUNTIF and SUMIF, if your criteria is text-related, you can use the question mark (?) and asterisk (*) as wildcard characters. A question mark stands in for a single character, an asterisk for a sequence of characters. And to search for an actual question mark or asterisk, use the tilde (~) before the character. So ~? and ~* to search for those actual symbols.

Finally, your ranges do not have to be the same size. Excel will start in the top left cell of the average range you tell it and define a range that matches the size and shape of the range you specified for the criteria.

I would recommend, however, that you define the appropriate range yourself rather than rely on Excel to do it for you.

THE AVERAGEIFS FUNCTION

Notation: AVERAGEIFS(average_range, criteria_range1, criteria1, [criteria_range2, criteria2],…)
Excel Definition: Finds average (arithmetic mean) for the cells specified by a given set of conditions or criteria.

AVERAGEIFS extends the functionality of AVERAGEIF to incorporate more than one criteria just like COUNTIFS and SUMIFS do for COUNTIF and SUMIF. It is available to users of Excel 2007 and later.

With AVERAGEIFS and AVERAGEIF you need to know which one you're going to use because the information for each function is provided in a different order. So for those of you who have access to AVERAGEIFS, I would recommend always using AVERAGEIFS since it can serve the same function as AVERAGEIF if you just limit it to one criteria.

The inputs for the function are the range of cells that contain the values you want to average followed by the range of cells for your first criteria and then the first criteria. If you have more than one criteria you then list the next range of cells and the next criteria and so on and so on.

Your criteria do not have to be of the same type and can reference numeric values (24 or "24"), cells (A1), expressions (">42"), or text ("how"). Cell references and numbers do not need to be in quotation marks, expressions and text references do.

With AVERAGEIFS your ranges must all be the same size and shape. (Unlike AVERAGEIF where Excel will figure out the average_range given a starting location.)

For a value to be included in the average calculation, all of the criteria you specify must be met.

Be careful with empty cells, blanks, or text values where numbers are expected as these may generate an error message rather than a calculation or may impact the calculation. (See the Excel help screen for the function for a full listing of the errors and adjustments that Excel makes. Always check a formula against a small sample of data to make sure you're getting the result you want.)

As with AVERAGEIF, you can use wildcards for text-based criteria.

An example of using AVERAGEIFS might be if you were looking at student grades and wanted to see average score across teacher name and student gender. Here's our data:

	A	B	C	D	E	F	G	H	I	J	K
1	Score	Teacher	Gender								
2	50	Smith	F								
3	49	Barker	M			Female		Male			
4	68	Vasquez	F			80.25	Smith	84.50			
5	75	Smith	M			90.00	Barker	68.67			
6	90	Barker	F			68.00	Vasquez	76.00			
7	94	Smith	M								
8	93	Barker	M			Cell F4:	=AVERAGEIFS($A$2:$A$13,$B$2:$B$13,G4,$C$2:$C$13,"F")				
9	91	Smith	F			Cell H4:	=AVERAGEIFS($A$2:$A$13,$B$2:$B$13,G4,$C$2:$C$13,"M")				
10	76	Vasquez	M								
11	82	Smith	F								
12	64	Barker	M								
13	98	Smith	F								

Test score is in Column A, teacher name is in Column B, student gender is in Column C. My full list of teacher names is in Column G. The formula I write in Cell F4 is:

=AVERAGEIFS($A$2:$A$13,$B$2:$B$13,G4,$C$2:$C$13,"F")

What that's saying is, average the values in Cells A2 through A13 where the values in Cells B2 through B13 are equal to the teacher name in Cell G4 and the gender of the student in Cells C2 through C13 is listed as F.

Because I used the $ signs there and a cell reference for teacher name, I can then just copy that formula to Cells F5 and F6 and it adjusts to calculate for each teacher.

I can then copy the formula to Cell H4, change the F at the end of the function to an M, and then copy that down to Cells H5 and H6.

Done. (Not statistically robust, but an interesting result.)

Okay. On to some Text functions now. These will be pretty simple and then we'll ramp back up with the Logical functions

THE UPPER FUNCTION

Notation: UPPER(text)
Excel Definition: Converts a text string to all uppercase letters.

The UPPER function has a very simple purpose, and that is to take a text entry and convert it to all uppercase letters.

So, for example, =UPPER("test") will return TEST. Or, if you had the word "test" in Cell B2 and you wrote =UPPER(B2) it would also return the value TEST.

You cannot reference more than once cell at a time using UPPER. However, you can combine the UPPER function with other functions to return a result that is in upper case letters.

For example,

=CONCATENATE(UPPER(B2)," ",UPPER(C2))

or

=UPPER(CONCATENATE(B2," ",C2))

would return the text in Cell B2 followed by a space and then by the text in Cell C2 all in upper case letters.

We'll talk about CONCATENATE later, don't worry. Just know for now that you can combine UPPER with it or any other function where that might make sense.

THE LOWER FUNCTION

Notation: LOWER(text)
Excel Definition: Converts all letters in a text string to lowercase.

In the same way that the UPPER function converts all letters in a text string to upper case, the LOWER function converts all letters in a text string to lower case.

So, for example, =LOWER("TEST") will return test. Or, if you had the word TEST in Cell B2 and you wrote =LOWER(B2) it would return the value test.

As with UPPER, with LOWER you cannot reference more than once cell at a time. However, LOWER can also be combined with other functions, which is probably the primary way you would use it. Either that or to convert imported data that's in the wrong format.

THE PROPER FUNCTION

Notation: PROPER(text)
Excel Definition: Converts a text string to proper case; the first letter in each word in uppercase, and all other letters to lowercase.

The PROPER function is much like the LOWER and the UPPER functions but in this case it converts text entries to Proper Case, which as you can see in the above definition means the first letter of each word will be capitalized but all other letters will not.

(Note that this is different from Title Case where most of the first letters are capitalized, but not all of them. Excel does not convert text to Title Case.)

For example, =PROPER("this is the entry to test") would return a value of This Is The Entry To Test. (Whereas with Title Case that would be This is the Entry to Test.)

As with UPPER and LOWER, you can either include the text to be converted in the formula itself like I did above or you can use a cell reference.

So =PROPER(B2) would convert the text in Cell B2 to proper case.

If you include the text within the formula, be sure to use quotation marks around the text.

Since there is not an option to convert text to Title Case within Excel, PROPER is as close as you can get. (If you were desperate, you could probably use PROPER to convert your text strings and then use a find/replace command for words like "the", "of", "in", "is", "and", etc. to replace the Proper Case versions with lower case versions to approximate Title Case.)

THE LEFT FUNCTION

Notation: LEFT(text, [num_chars])
Excel Definition: Returns the specified number of characters from the start of a text string.

The LEFT function allows you to extract the left-most portion of a text string. This can be a useful function if you only want a portion of a standardized entry. For example, for a driver's license number that starts with a two-digit year, then a dash, then the license number, to extract the year portion, you could use =LEFT(B2,2) assuming the value was in Cell B2. That would give you just the year portion of that license number.

Note that the definition says it works on a text string, but I was able to also get it to work on a number. So =LEFT(1234,2) returns 12.

You can accomplish the same thing with Text to Columns using Fixed Width, but LEFT is a better option when all you want is that one portion of the entry and you don't need the rest of it.

Other identifiers that might be similarly structured include customer identification numbers and social security numbers.

The number of characters specified must be greater than or equal to zero.

If the number of characters you specify is greater than the length of the text entry, Excel will return the full text entry.

If you omit the number of characters, Excel will extract the left-most character only. So =LEFT("test") will return a result of t.

For languages such as Chinese, Japanese, and Korean you may need to use LEFTB instead and specify the number of bytes rather than the number of characters.

THE RIGHT FUNCTION

Notation: RIGHT(text, [num_chars])
Excel Definition: Returns the specified number of characters from the end of a text string.

The RIGHT function allows you to extract the right-most portion of a text string. Just as with the LEFT function, this can be a useful function if you only want a portion of a standardized entry.

For example, =RIGHT(B2,4) would extract the last four digits of a social security number that had been entered in Cell B2.

Again, as with LEFT, you could accomplish the same thing with Text to Columns using Fixed Width, but this approach only extracts the portion that you need rather than breaking the existing entry into sections. Other identifiers that might be similarly structured include customer identification numbers or driver's license numbers.

The number of characters you specify must be greater than or equal to zero. If the number of characters you specify is greater than the number of characters in the entry, the function will return the entire text entry.

If you omit the number of characters, Excel will assume the value is 1 and return the last character in the entry. So =RIGHT("try") will return a value of y.

Entries that are in Chinese, Korean, or Japanese may require the use of RIGHTB instead. If so, you'd specify a number of bytes instead of a number of characters.

THE MID FUNCTION

Notation: MID(text, start_num, num_chars)
Excel Definition: Returns the characters from the middle of a text string, given a starting position and length.

The MID function works much like the LEFT and RIGHT functions except it extracts characters from the middle of an entry. Because of this, it requires one more input, the start number. So you have to tell Excel which character in your string should be the first character pulled and then how many characters you want after that.

For example, for a social security number if you want the middle two digits of the value stored in Cell B2 you would use =MID(B2,5,2) assuming the number was written as XXX-XX-XXXX.

Be sure to count each space, dash, etc. in your determination of the start number.

If your start number is greater than the number of characters in your referenced text, Excel will return an empty text entry.

If you ask for more characters to be returned than exist, Excel will return what there is. So =MID("advice",3,7) will returned vice even though that's only four characters.

Your start number must be equal to or greater than 1. Your number of characters must be equal to or greater than zero.

If you are working with entries in Chinese, Japanese, or Korean you may need to use MIDB instead and specify a number of bytes rather than a number of characters.

THE TRIM FUNCTION

Notation: TRIM(text)

Excel Definition: Removes all spaces from a text string except for single spaces between words.

The TRIM function can come in very handy if you're trying to clean up text entries that are messy.

For example, if I did some sort of merge of a list of names (perhaps using CONCATENATE) to create a list of entries that had first name followed by a space followed by middle name followed by a space followed by last name followed by a space and then followed by a suffix such as Esq. or Jr., I would very likely end up with a list of entries with extra spaces in it.

Because for every entry that didn't have a middle name or suffix there would be an unwanted space.

So I might have "Albert Jones " as one of my entries. There's an extra space there between Albert and Jones because there was no middle name and an extra space after Jones because there was no suffix.

To remove those extra spaces, you can use the TRIM function. If that entry was in Cell B2, I'd just write =TRIM(B2).

Done. My new entry would be "Albert Jones".

I could also combine this with CONCATENATE so that the trimming was done at the same time I created the entry, which saves the use of an extra column.

In that case I would list the TRIM function first and in the parens for the TRIM function I would write my CONCATENATE function. So

$$=TRIM(CONCATENATE(\ldots))$$

Where the … represents the values for the CONCATENATE function.

TRIM also works with text pasted directly into the function as long as you use quotation marks around the text. For example, =TRIM("Albert Jones ") with the extra spaces would return Albert Jones without the extra spaces.

Also, remember that when you use TRIM it's still a formula. To get just the text entry and not keep the formula you need to copy your data and then paste special – values.

You probably won't need to use TRIM often, but it's very useful when you do need it. Also, if you're pulling information off a website and have issues, see the TRIM Excel Help text for more guidance.

THE CONCATENATE FUNCTION

Notation: CONCATENATE(text1, [text2],…)
Excel Definition: Joins several text strings into one text string.

I've referred to it a couple times now, so we better talk about it. The CONCATENATE function is one I use often. It lets me take separate elements, such as first and last name, and create one entry that combines those elements.

For example, on a recent work project I was given a list of employee names that was in first name and then last name order. (Mark Smith, Betsy Poole, etc.) But some of the first names were nicknames or shortened names so it was always hard to find someone on that list. I'd look for Bob and he'd be listed under Robert or Robert and he'd be listed under Bob.

So I decided to redo the list with last name comma first name instead.

I used Text to Columns to separate first name and last name and then CONCATENATE to recombine the entries in the order I wanted. (E.g., Smith, Mark) This made searching the list much, much easier.

That's just one way to use CONCATENATE.

You can use it to combine any combination of values you want. And, because it's a formula, you can do this for multiple rows of data very easily.

Now, a few things to know about CONCATENATE before you start:

The inputs into your CONCATENATE function can be a cell reference (B1), a number (32 or "32"), or a text value ("entry"). If it's text it must have quotes around it. If it's a number the quotes are optional. For a cell reference, do not use quotes.

You can have up to 255 elements in a CONCATENATE formula and a total of 8,192 characters. (At least in Excel 2013 you can. Why you'd do that, I'm not sure, but it is possible.)

If you want a space or any sort of punctuation in your final result you need to include that in the CONCATENATE formula.

So, with the example above where I wanted last name comma first name, I had to write that as:

=CONCATENATE(B1,", ",A1)

Let's break that down a bit because it's a little hard to see what's happening there.

The first text entry I wanted was the value in Cell B1. So that's what I wrote after the opening paren.

Then I used a comma to separate that entry from the next entry.

So far we have:

$$=CONCATENATE(B1,$$

After that first comma I needed to tell Excel to add a comma and a space between the last name and the first name. Because that wasn't a cell reference I had to put quotes around it. So we end up with an opening quote, followed by a comma and a space, followed by a closing quote. Which is how we get the ", " portion of that formula.

That's our second entry in the formula. Since we have a third entry we want to include, we follow it with a comma.

At that point we have:

$$=CONCATENATE(B1,", ",$$

The third entry in the formula is another cell reference, so we just add that and close it all out with a closing paren.

And we get:

$$=CONCATENATE(B1,", ",A1)$$

There is a way to get the same result as the CONCATENATE function that doesn't require a function by using ampersands (&) between elements.

So if I write

$$=B1 \& ", " \& A1$$

that gives the same result as

$$=CONCATENATE(B1,", ",A1)$$

If you get a NAME#? error this is usually because you failed to put quotation marks around a text element in your formula.

Also, I should note here that Excel in their infinite wisdom—not—has added a new function CONCAT to Excel 2016, Excel Mobile, and Excel Online to replace CONCATENATE. They now warn that CONCATENATE may not be available in future versions of Excel. (Because that'll make users happy, to have to write something in two formats to support users using old versions of Excel and then newer versions of Excel.)

So be aware of this and know that you may have to adjust at some point to using the CONCAT function instead of the CONCATENATE function. Also, if that ever does happen and you're working with users in an older version of Excel know that you may have compatibility issues as a result.

That's CONCATENATE. Let's move on to TEXT next.

THE TEXT FUNCTION

Notation: TEXT(value, format_text)
Excel Definition: Converts a value to text in a specific number format.

The TEXT function is an interesting one. Because it really has two completely different uses. (In my opinion.) So let's start with the usage that's a lot like using CONCATENATE.

Basically, you can use TEXT to combine numbers with text or to specify how those numbers are formatted. So if you have a column of numbers, 1, 2, 3, etc. and you want to turn those into a column of entries that say $1.00 per unit, $2.00 per unit, $3.00 per unit, etc., TEXT is the easiest way to do that.

In that example, you would write

=TEXT(A1,"$0.00") & " per unit"

where the value being transformed is in Cell A1. That tells Excel to format the number in Cell A1 with a dollar sign and two decimal places and then to add a space and the text "per unit" to the end of the entry.

Now, the part of TEXT that interests me is its ability to extract information from a date. Using TEXT you can take a date, like 4/4/2018, and you can have Excel return for you the name of the day of the week or the month associated with that date. So "Wednesday" or "April".

I find that very useful, and recently used it when I was trying to create a pivot table with day of the week across the top but only had dates to work with.

To extract the name of the day of the week, use =TEXT(A1,"dddd").

To extract the name of the month, use =TEXT(A1,"mmmm")

You can also extract the abbreviated month or day of the week as well as just the number of the day or month by using a different number of d's or m's in your formula.

If you're really really interested in using the TEXT function I suggest reading the help text for the function, because Excel provides a seventeen-tab worksheet on how to use it. Since covering that here would overwhelm the other content in this guide, I'm just going to cover some high points.

Be careful when using TEXT to create number formats, because it is possible to create entries that no one would want. You can end up with an entry like where there's a number followed by a period and then nothing after that period. (Who would want that? Not me.) Or you can get a format where you have a number followed by a period followed by a space and then followed by another number. Again, no one wants that.

But Excel will let you do it. So if you use this function you need to be very careful to check your results to make sure you got it right.

Also, remember that this is a text function. So once you use it, the entry you create is text not a number. If you intend to do any sort of calculations on your values, you should retain a version of those values somewhere that are still formatted as numbers or do all of your analysis first.

If you aren't really interested in the TEXT function, I'd suggest you stop here. But if you want to dig in a little further, we can continue.

* * *

First, if you're not sure how to write a format that you want to use on a number, you can click on a cell and then go to the Format Cells dialogue box (Ctrl + 1 or right-click Format Cells), and then go to the Number tab. If the type of number format you want already exists, like Percentage, click on it first and then go to Custom and that format will be the one that's selected under Custom.

See above where the notation selected is now "0.00%" under Custom?

(Of course, if that's what you wanted, you could just format your cells as a percentage and be done. But I assume you're using TEXT because you want to combine that number formatting with text. So this approach allows you to pull that notation for inclusion in your TEXT formula and know that it will work.)

As an example:

=TEXT(A1,"0.00%")

will format the value in Cell A1 as a percentage and including & " Completion" in that formula:

=TEXT(A1,"0.00%") & " Completion"

will return "50.00% Completion" as your result, for example, where the value in Cell A1 is 50.

Be sure to put quotes around the cell notation when you use it in your TEXT function.

Also, Excel may reject your format even if it's one you pulled from the Format Cells dialogue box, because Excel does not accept all of those formats as valid when used in the TEXT function.

If you want to build a cell notation from scratch, here are a few tips:

A comma between either pound signs (#) or zeros (0) will be treated as an indication that you should include a comma to separate out your thousands.

If you end your entry with a comma then Excel will round that number to the nearest 1000s. (In other countries, you may actually need to do this with a period instead of a comma.)

So =TEXT(12000000, "#,###") returns 12,000,000.

But =TEXT(12000000, "#,###,") returns 12,000 because the comma at the end says to round to the nearest thousand.

And =TEXT(12000000, "#,###,,") returns 12 because it has two commas at the end so you round to the nearest thousand twice.

If you use zeros (0) in your notation, Excel will force all entries to have that many numbers or zeros even if the number wouldn't otherwise.

So =TEXT(4,"0.0000") will return 4.0000 and =TEXT(4,"0000") will return 0004 with three zeros in front of the four.

(This is one way to fix a situation where Excel removed an initial 0 from a long number string. The other way to prevent that is to use the single quote mark before you enter the value.)

You can also use pound signs (#). In that case, Excel will round the number to that many places if the number is longer, but it won't force a number to have that many digits.

So =TEXT(4,"#.####") will return the number 4 followed by a period.

(Remember how I said you can get bad formatting with TEXT. This is how.)

Since it's a whole number no zeros are added. In this case, to have a "good" format you'd probably want something like =TEXT(4,"#.0###") so that you have 4.0 rather than that 4 with a period after it.

For comparison's sake, =TEXT(4,"####") returns 4 as the value. No added zeros before the number.

Bottom line here: TEXT can be useful for formatting existing numbers and combining those with text, but you need to be very, very careful how you do so and it's probably best to liberally borrow from Excel's existing number formatting for your notation.

It is also a very convenient and helpful way to extract the day of the week or month from a date. (It can also extracts hours, minutes, and seconds if needed.)

If you're going to work with it, use the Excel Help screen to find the notation you need.

Now on to a few Date & Time functions.

THE TODAY FUNCTION

Notation: TODAY()
Excel Definition: Returns the current date formatted as a date.

The TODAY function is very simple and basic. If you need today's date formatted as a date, you just enter =TODAY() into a cell and that's what you'll get.

Now, you might be asking yourself why you'd bother doing something like this. I mean, can't you just type in today's date? Yes, you can.

But the reason I use TODAY is because I'm usually using it in conjunction with a worksheet that's calculating days until something happens. So let's say you want to track which of your customer invoices are past thirty days. In other words, who should've paid you by now.

You can have a cell in your worksheet that uses TODAY so that you never have to re-enter today's date when making your calculations. It will update each time you open your worksheet. And then you can combine that with a calculation that looks at date billed to calculate how many days past due someone is on their payment. That, too, will automatically update each time you open your worksheet.

You can also use TODAY directly in a formula.

(But remember that best practice about having all of your assumptions visible. If you bury TODAY in a formula and someone doesn't realize it they may believe the values are static when in fact they will change each day as that value updates.)

So Option 1 is to put =TODAY() into Cell A1 and then have the formula =A1-C3 where A1 is today's date and C3 is the date the customer was invoiced.

Option 2 is to put

$$=TODAY()-C3$$

into a cell where C3 is the date the customer was invoiced. Both work.

As long as you format your cell as a number it should return the number of day's difference between the two dates.

Now you do have to be a little careful about dates in Excel.

Excel behind the scenes is storing each date as a number and that numbering starts with January 1, 1900. So if you ever find yourself dealing with dates prior to January 1, 1900 (which I did once when dealing with incorporation dates for companies), you will have some issues using Excel. I once imported data into Excel and it converted dates from the 1700s and 1800s into modern dates. Not something I wanted and not something that was obvious when the dates were formatted with just a two-digit year (1/1/18).

THE NOW FUNCTION

Notation: NOW()
Excel Definition: Returns the current date and time formatted as a date and time.

The NOW function is just like the TODAY function, except it also returns the current time of day. According to Excel the format the date displays in will be the format for your local date and time settings.

So if I use =TODAY() my computer displays 5/12/2018, and if I format that to show the time of day it displays as 5/12/18 0:00, so midnight of May 12th.

If I use =NOW() my computer displays 5/12/18 8:48 because it's currently eight forty-eight in the morning here as I type this. If I were to use NOW later in the day I might see 5/12/18 14:23 which would be two twenty-three in the afternoon.

You will not normally be able to tell the difference between the two entries unless you are using a date format in Excel that shows time of day. But if you are doing calculations on dates in Excel this could be an important difference.

Usually I just need to use TODAY for my purposes because I'm dealing with number of days between two dates, but if minutes and hours matter to your calculation, then you should use NOW instead.

Just keep in mind with NOW that just like with TODAY it will continue to update to the current time when your worksheet is recalculated. This happens when you press F9, do another calculation in the worksheet, or when you open the worksheet.

If you need an exact time to be preserved and used in the future, you need to take steps to lock that value in place. For example, by copying and using paste special – values.

(If you've ever used one of those memo templates in Word that autofill the date for you, you will understand why this can be an issue. You write the memo, save it, open it two weeks later, and suddenly it's dated for today instead of the date you wrote it. So think this through if you're using NOW or TODAY for documentation purposes.)

If you're interested in how to use NOW with addition and subtraction the Excel Help screen for the function gives a few examples.

Basically, with respect to time, Excel converts the hours in a day into decimals. So .5 is the equivalent of 12 hours, .25 is the equivalent of 6 hours, etc. You can say something like =NOW()-.5 to return a time 12 hours ago. Or =NOW()+7 to return a time that is exactly seven days from now. Be sure you include the () with the function name or it won't work.

THE IF FUNCTION

Notation: IF(logical_test, [value_if_true], [value if false])
Excel Definition: Checks whether a condition is met, and returns one value if TRUE, and another value if FALSE.

Now let's talk the IF function.

I love the IF function. It is probably the most valuable function to me. And it's not because of its most basic use which is to say, "If X happens return Y, otherwise return Z." That's pretty simple. Powerful but simple.

No, what I love the IF function for is the fact that I can nest them. So I can say, "If X happens, return Y. If X doesn't happen, but G does, then return H. And if neither X nor G happens, then return Z." And you can keep going and going and going with that until you have twenty possible outcomes.

(Maybe not for those of you in older versions of Excel. I used to run out of how many IF functions I could nest long before I was done and then I'd have to use an IF function that referenced another IF function to get what I wanted. But in newer versions of Excel that is no longer an issue. You can nest up to 64 IF functions in Excel 2013, although that would probably get highly unwieldy.)

So a basic IF function goes IF-THEN-ELSE or IF-THEN-OTHERWISE.

A nested IF function replaces that THEN or that ELSE with another IF Function.

Let's walk through some examples. First we'll build an IF function to give free shipping to any customer who spends at least $25. Any customer who spends less than $25 will pay 5% in shipping costs.

To calculate our shipping cost, we write that as

$$=IF(A1>=25,0,A1*.05)$$

Let's break that down.

The first part, our IF part, is A1>=25. We're saying that if the customer's purchase (in Cell A1) is greater than (>) OR equal to (=) 25 then we want the first outcome.

The second part, our THEN part or first outcome, is 0. If the customer's purchase is equal to or greater than 25, then don't charge for shipping.

That leaves us with the third part, our ELSE part. And that's A1*.05.

Notice that for the calculation A1*.05 we don't have to use quotation marks. (Unlike some other functions where you do.)

Also note here that we are calculating the *shipping charge*, not the customer's transaction cost. If we wanted the total customer cost we would use =IF(A1>=25,A1,A1*1.05)

So that was a basic IF function. One condition, two possible outcomes.

The complexity level ratchets up when you start to nest IF functions. Let's look at the basic format of an IF function again.

It's IF-THEN-ELSE, right? IF x, THEN y, ELSE z. Or IF-THEN-OTHERWISE. IF x, THEN y, OTHERWISE z.

When you nest IF Functions you're basically just replacing that y or that z with another IF function. So it becomes IF x, THEN other IF function, ELSE z.

And you can do that for layer after layer after layer.

The example I used in *Intermediate Excel* is a customer discount that escalates as customers spend more and more money. Spend $150, get $20 off. Spend $75, get $15 off. Etc. Let's look at a simplified version of that example that has just two tiers. If a customer spends at least $25 they get $5 off. If they spend $100, they get $10 off.

Here we go:

	A	B	C
1	Customer Spend	Rebate	
2	$25.00	$5.00	
3	$100.00	$10.00	
4			
5			
6	Order Amount	Rebate Amount	Formula in Column B
7	$10.00	$0.00	=IF(A7>=$A$3,$B$3,IF(A7>=$A$2,$B$2,0))
8	$25.00	$5.00	=IF(A8>=$A$3,$B$3,IF(A8>=$A$2,$B$2,0))
9	$50.00	$5.00	=IF(A9>=$A$3,$B$3,IF(A9>=$A$2,$B$2,0))
10	$100.00	$10.00	=IF(A10>=$A$3,$B$3,IF(A10>=$A$2,$B$2,0))
11	$125.00	$10.00	=IF(A11>=$A$3,$B$3,IF(A11>=$A$2,$B$2,0))

The formula for Row 7 is:

$$=IF(A7>=\$A\$3,\$B\$3,IF(A7>=\$A\$2,\$B\$2,0))$$

Let's walk through what that's saying.

First, if the value in Cell A7 (the customer order amount) is greater than or equal to the value in Cell A3 (the highest discount tier) then the customer gets the discount in Cell B3 (the $10 discount).

That's =IF(A7>=$A$3,$B$3,

Now, if this were a simple IF function, the next input to the function would be a value or cell reference. But because we're nesting IF functions, the next input is another IF function:

$$IF(A7>=\$A\$2,\$B\$2,0)$$

This one says that if the value in Cell A7 is greater than the value in Cell A2 (we already know it's not greater than the value in Cell A3 because Excel didn't return the value in Cell B3), then return the value in Cell B2. And if that's also not the case, then just return a value of zero.

If you had more levels that you wanted to consider you'd replace that zero with yet another IF function.

Now, note here that I started with the highest discount and worked my way downward. You could start at the bottom and work your way upward as well. Either direction will work. They'll just look different.

What I've found works best is to build a nested IF function so that I'm closing out all of my IF functions at once at the end. That means that if I build a nested IF function in the "correct" direction, that IF function will end with closing parens for however many IF functions I used. (See how up above there were two closing parens at the end?)

Now, I'll tell you. Most times I build a nested IF function it doesn't work on the first try. I always mess something up.

But that's okay. That's life.

When that happens, as it will, the first thing I check is that I have the right number of parens and that they're in the right spot. So after every single IF there should be an opening paren. And for every opening paren there should be one closing paren. They should all match up. That usually takes care of the "too many arguments" error message.

I also test the formula to make sure that I'm getting the results I expect at each threshold. So is it giving me "greater than" or is it giving me "greater than or equal to"? Are any of my conditions being skipped over or returning an incorrect response?

If that's the case, then the best way to address the issue is to replace everything else in your IF function with a placeholder and to test each section of the IF function in isolation.

So I don't try to decipher this all at once:

$$-IF(A22>\$A\$2,IF(A22>\$A\$3,IF(A22>\$A\$4,IF(A22>\$A\$5,$$
$$IF(A22>\$A\$5,\$B\$5),\$B\$4),\$B\$3),\$B\$2),0)$$

(This is an example written in what I find the harder format for nested IF functions because each new IF function is added in the middle of the formula rather than the end.)

What I do is remove everything except the first IF function. So I take that mess up there and I make it:

$$=IF(A22>\$A\$2,"THEN",0)$$

And I ask myself if that makes sense. If it does, then I check next part:

$$=IF(A22>\$A\$3,"THEN",\$B\$2)$$

Does that make sense?

I just keep going through one step at a time to make sure it's all working the way it should. And eventually I find where the error is.

Remember with nested IF functions: slow and steady wins the race. Take it one step at a time. Test your possible outcomes. Don't get frustrated. Draw a diagram if you have to.

Next we'll cover VLOOKUP which is what all my programmer/computer savvy friends swear by instead of using nested IF functions.

THE VLOOKUP FUNCTION

Notation: VLOOKUP(lookup_value, table_array, col_index_num, [range_lookup])
Excel Definition: Looks for a value in the leftmost column of a table, and then returns a value in the same row from a column you specify. By default, the table must be sorted in an ascending order.

Full disclosure here. I hate VLOOKUP. Every time I've wanted to use it it's caused me more problems than it's been worth. But I think if you were to set out to use VLOOKUP (as opposed to my trying to fit it into an existing scenario after the fact) that it could be very useful. And Excel (and my computer programmer friends) certainly thinks it's a better choice than using nested IF functions.

So if you're not like me, and you don't find it fun to nest six or seven levels of IF functions, this might be the better solution for you.

To effectively use VLOOKUP you need a data table that has values that can be looked up and values that are returned when there's a match. This data table needs to be sorted in ascending order. (That's the mistake I usually make. I want to look up values in a table of customer data that's in any old order and VLOOKUP can't do that.)

What VLOOKUP is good at is using a reference table, like our discounting example above. Something like this:

	I	J
1	VLOOKUP TABLE	
2	Customer Spend	Rebate
3	$0.00	$0.00
4	$25.00	$5.00
5	$50.00	$10.00
6	$75.00	$15.00
7	$150.00	$20.00

It can take each value you give it, compare it to the values in that reference table, and return a value for you based on where your data falls in the reference table.

The first input for VLOOKUP is the value from your data that you want to look up. So, in this example, the customer's transaction amount. I have a customer who paid $60. Do they get a discount? And, if so, how much?

The next input for VLOOKUP is a reference to the cell range where Excel needs to look for that value and where the value you want it to return is. So this isn't a single column. It's multiple columns.

In our example, just two. But it could be ten. Or twenty. Just not one. Because you need what you're looking up and then you need what value you're returning. That's two columns, minimum.

The left-most column of that range MUST be the value you're looking up. And then the value you're returning MUST be somewhere to the right of that. (These are the reasons VLOOKUP never works for me. Because my data isn't always built like they want it to be. Don't be me. Think about these things in advance.)

The third entry in a VLOOKUP is which column in the range of cells you gave in the second entry contains the value you want. Column 1 contains what you're using for your search. Count from there to find your column number for your result. In this table above, our number is 2 because it's the second column in our range.

Finally, you need to tell Excel whether it's looking for an exact match (0/FALSE) or an approximate match (1/TRUE). If it's an exact match, you'll only get a value returned when what you're looking up matches an entry in the table exactly. If it's an approximate match you'll get a result for all entries and your value will be determined based on the table sort and where that value falls in the range of values.

Let's look at the full table I used for discounting in *Intermediate Excel*.

It turns out we need to change our table to get this to work. When I tried using the table I'd used for the IF functions, I had an error for the lowest tier. So I had to put in a zero customer spend, zero discount row to make this work. Here we go:

	I	J
1	VLOOKUP TABLE	
2	Customer Spend	Rebate
3	$0.00	$0.00
4	$25.00	$5.00
5	$50.00	$10.00
6	$75.00	$15.00
7	$150.00	$20.00
8		
9	Cell J11 =VLOOKUP(I11,$I$3:$J$7,2,TRUE)	
10	Order Amount	Rebate Amount
11	$5.00	$0.00
12	$25.00	$5.00
13	$40.00	$5.00
14	$50.00	$10.00
15	$60.00	$10.00
16	$75.00	$15.00
17	$140.00	$15.00
18	$150.00	$20.00

Let's look at the sample for Row 11 that's shown in Row 9.

$$=VLOOKUP(I11,\$I\$3:\$J\$7,2,TRUE)$$

That first entry, I11 is where we have the customer transaction amount of $5.00.

The second entry $I$3:$J$7 is where we have our discount table. Note that the first column in the range, Column I is where we have the value we want to look up. And that the range contains the column, Column J, where the value we want to return is stored.

Note, too, that I did not include the header row in the provided range. (That returns an error message.)

Also, note that the table is sorted in ascending order. If it isn't VLOOKUP does not work correctly.

The third entry is where we tell Excel which column to look in for the results In this case that's 2, the second column in our range.

And finally, the fourth entry tells Excel whether we're looking for exact matches to the entries in the table or whether an approximate match is okay.

Since we have ranges we want to pull from ($0-$24.99 gets no discount, $25 to $49.99 gets $5, etc.) we say "TRUE" to allow for approximate results.

If I were to change that to FALSE, I would get a bunch of #N/A results except for rows where customer spend was $25, $50, $75, or $150.

Now, compare that to what we had to use to build a nested IF function that does the same thing:

$$=IF(A11>=\$A\$6,\$B\$6,IF(A11>=\$A\$5,\$B\$5,IF(A11>=\$A\$4,\$B\$4,IF(A11>=\$A\$3,\$B\$3,0))))$$

Clearly it's easier to write the VLOOKUP function to do this. But remember that I built that table so that VLOOKUP would work with it.

As I said above, I run into issues using VLOOKUP because I want to use it on unsorted data or on data that has the value I want to pull to the left of the lookup value in my lookup table. So for me it's easier to write a nested IF function than it is to rearrange my data so that it works with VLOOKUP. I suspect I am in the minority there.

Just think of nested IF functions as the way to do VLOOKUP without all the pesky rules. But because there are no rules, you have to do a lot more of the heavy lifting.

A few more points:

Excel cautions that numbers or dates stored as text may produce unexpected results and so may text entries that have inconsistent usage of spaces or quote marks.

If the data table you're using for your lookup values is large or complex, be very, very careful that the results you get are what you expect. And absolutely be sure to sort your data table in ascending order.

Also check, double-check, and check again.

And one final point.

With an IF function to change the IF formula to adjust for whether you want your criteria to be "a customer spent $25 or more" versus "a customer spent over $25" you adjust the formula from >= to >. With VLOOKUP, you'll need to adjust your lookup table not your formula. So instead of $25.00 in the table, we'd have $25.01 for a situation where customers get the discount if they spend over $25 as opposed to $25 or more.

OK. That's IF functions and VLOOKUP. Let's talk about some functions that on their surface are very basic, but when combined with other functions can be much more powerful. That's AND and OR.

THE AND FUNCTION

Notation: AND(logical1, [logical2],…)
Excel Definition: Checks whether all arguments are TRUE, and returns TRUE if all arguments are TRUE.

At its core, the AND function is very basic. You use it to determine whether more than one criteria is met. So, is that value greater than 10 AND less than 20? Is that customer from Alaska AND has he bought Widgets?

It doesn't have to be just two criteria either. You can use more than two with an AND function. (Although the help text for the function doesn't say exactly how many you can use.)

In my numeric example above, you would write that as

$$=AND(A1>10,A1<20)$$

If the value in Cell A1 was greater than 10 and less than 20 Excel would return a value of TRUE. Or in the second example I gave, you could write that as

$$=AND(A1="Alaska",B1="Widget")$$

(Assuming A1 contained the state information and B1 contained the product information). Again, if both criteria were met, Excel would return a value of TRUE.

In addition to working with numbers, like the first example above, and text references, like the second example above, AND works with cell references. So:

$$=AND(A1>D1,A1<D2)$$

looks to see if the value in Cell A1 is greater than the value in Cell D1 and also less than the value in Cell D2.

I rarely if ever use AND on a standalone basis. You could, like I showed in the examples above, but what I've used it for instead was if I had an IF function where I needed two criteria met.

For example, if I wanted all customers who bought Widgets and live in Alaska to qualify for 50% off their purchase amount. I could write an equation to calculate total cost as:

$$=IF(AND(A1="Alaska",B1="Widget"),C1*0.5,C1)$$

where A1 contains their state, B1 the product they've bought, and C1 contains the purchase amount.

In that example, I just replaced the first portion of the IF function with:

$$AND(A1="Alaska",B1="Widget")$$

I don't use AND often, but when I do it's very helpful. Same with OR which we'll discuss next.

THE OR FUNCTION

Notation: OR(logical1, [logical2],…)
Excel Definition: Checks whether any of the arguments are TRUE, and returns TRUE or FALSE. Returns FALSE only if all arguments are FALSE.

The OR function is similar to the AND function except it doesn't require that all of the conditions are met to return a TRUE value. With OR if one of the conditions in the list is met, then the value is TRUE.

Say, for example, I want to identify all of my customers who are in the states of Florida, Georgia, and North Carolina because I have a special promotion running in those states. I could write that as =OR(A1="Florida",A1="Georgia",A1="North Carolina") and if the value in Cell A1 was any of those (Florida, Georgia, or North Carolina), Excel would return a value of TRUE.

If none of the conditions were met, Excel would return a value of FALSE.

Once more, this is one I rarely use as a standalone, but it is nice to use it with an IF function. So say I was running a price promotion in those three states, I could write an IF function that says,

=IF(OR(A1="Florida",A1="Georgia",A1="North Carolina"),C1*.5,C1)

to give a 50% discount to any customer in one of those three states.

Like with AND, you can use text criteria (like above), numeric criteria, or cell references.

So =OR(A1=C1,A1=C3) would check to see if the value in Cell A1 was the same as the value in Cell C1 OR the value in Cell C3.

And =OR(A1=5,A1=10) would check to see if the value in Cell A1 was equal to 5 OR 10.

This is another one you probably won't use often, but will appreciate when you need it.

THE TRUE FUNCTION

Notation: TRUE()
Excel Definition: Returns the logical value TRUE.

When I was working on this guide I found myself occasionally needing a cell to return a value of TRUE or FALSE to test some of the different functions. Simply typing TRUE into the cell didn't always work, so I found myself using TRUE and its counterpart, FALSE.

If you use it, be sure to include the parens () or Excel may think you're trying to reference a named range.

You should also be able to just type TRUE and get the same result, but that didn't always seem to work for me.

I would likely use TRUE and FALSE in other functions, like IF functions rather than having the function return a value of 0 or " " if I were then going to apply a function such as AVERAGEA to the range.

According to Excel, TRUE exists primarily for compatibility with other spreadsheet programs.

THE FALSE FUNCTION

Notation: FALSE()
Excel Definition: Returns the logical value FALSE.

As I mentioned under the description for TRUE, when I was working on this guide I found myself occasionally needing a cell to return a value of TRUE or FALSE to test some of the different functions. Simply typing FALSE into the cell didn't always work even though it's supposed to, so I found myself using the FALSE function and its counterpart, TRUE.

Be sure if you're using the function that you include the parens, so write =FALSE() or if it's in the midst of another function write it as FALSE() with the parens after the text.

According to Excel FALSE exists primarily for compatibility with other spreadsheet programs.

THE NA FUNCTION

Notation: NA()
Excel Definition: Returns the error value #N/A (value not available)

You can use the NA function to mark empty cells. This avoids the issue of inadvertently including empty cells in your calculations.

A friend of mine suggested including it in this guide because he recently had a scenario where he was generating results using an IF function and then graphing those results. When his results generated an empty cell or a null value Excel tried to include those entries in the graph. He found that using NA fixed that problem, because Excel does not graph #N/A values.

To do this, you could write something like this:

=IF(A1>10,5,NA())

In this case, if A1 is greater than 10, Excel returns a value of 5 but if it isn't Excel returns a value of #N/A.

Be sure to use the empty parens as I did in the example above or Excel won't recognize it as the NA function.

THE RAND FUNCTION

Notation: RAND()

Excel Definition: Returns a random number greater than or equal to 0 and less than 1, evenly distributed. (Changes on recalculation.)

For some types of calculations, you need to have a random start.

For example, if I want to sample a series of transactions and be able to extrapolate my results to that entire population of transactions, I need to start at a random point and then take every nth transaction from that point forward until I've worked my way through the entire sample back to my starting point.

(The n is usually determined by taking your total population and dividing it by your sample size. Where I used to work we'd often take a sample of 60 transactions. So if my population was 10,000 transactions then I'd want every 167th transaction until I reached my sample of 60. You can use a function like RAND to make sure that you're starting at a random point, because starting at Transaction 1 each time isn't truly random.)

If I say =RAND()*10000, that gives me my starting point. Actually, for this example, it would be best to use =INT(RAND()*10000) to make sure that it gives me an integer instead of a decimal value.

Be careful with RAND, though. Because every time you press F9, make a new calculation in your worksheet, or reopen your worksheet it will calculate a new random value. And once it does that there's no way to go back to your prior value. Ctrl + Z will not work. That number is gone and it's not coming back.

So if you do this and you need to record the random number Excel generates, which you likely will, use copy and paste special – values to store the value as a number. (Or build a process that acts on that value as soon as it's generated.) Just know that as soon as you paste special – values the original value is going to change and will no longer match the number you just pasted.

THE RANDBETWEEN FUNCTION

Notation: RANDBETWEEN(bottom, top)
Excel Definition: Returns a random number between the numbers you specify.

RANDBETWEEN is much like RAND, except you can specify a range of numbers for it to choose between and the number returned will always be an integer (whole number).

As with RAND, every time the worksheet is opened or you hit F9 or choose recalculate, a new random value will be generated. So if you need to keep your number, generate the value and then convert it to just a number using paste special – values.

We could've used RANDBETWEEN for the example I gave above for RAND.

=RANDBETWEEN(1,10000)

would choose a random transaction to start with in our range of ten thousand transactions.

Another example of when you might use this is a jury duty selection. Say today's jurors have numbers assigned between 12345 and 23456, you could use

=RANDBETWEEN(12345,23456)

to randomly select the jurors who will serve on a jury.

If you need ten jurors, you can just copy and paste the formula until you have ten entries. (For small population sizes it is possible to repeat a value.) Your other option is to hit F9 to recalculate and record the values returned until you have the number of values you need for your sample. Just remember to write each one down or copy it over as a number before you calculate the next one.

THE RANK FUNCTION

Notation: RANK(number, ref, [order])
Excel Definition: Returns the rank of a number in a list of numbers: its size relative to other values in the list.

According to Excel this function only exists in current versions of Excel for compatibility with Excel 2007 or earlier. In Excel 2013 or later this function has been replaced with RANK.AVG and RANK.EQ.

As its definition says, RANK tells you the rank of a number within a range of numbers. Is it the 5th value in the list? The 10th? RANK will tell you.

The first input into the function is the number you're analyzing.

The next input is the overall range of numbers you want to compare it to. (The number can be pulled from the reference range and probably will be in most instances.)

The final input, order, tells Excel which way to rank things. If you omit it, which you can, or use a zero (0), then Excel will rank the value based on descending order. If you use a one (1) or any other number other than zero, Excel will rank the value based on ascending order.

I used a range of numbers from 1 through 15 and had Excel rank the 6 in that range.

=RANK(6,J1:J15,0) returned a value of 10 regardless of how the reference range was sorted.

=RANK(6,J1:J15) returned the same value.

So in those two instances, 15 was considered the best rank, 1 the worst.

=RANK(6,A1:A15,1) returned a value of 6 regardless of how the reference range was sorted.

In that instance, 1 was considered the best rank, 15 the worst.

I found this counterintuitive because my default is to always think of 1 as the best rank. So if you're like me you should test your data on an obvious sample to see if the rank you're getting makes sense before you apply it to a full range of data. If it's backwards from what you expected, then change the order input in your formula.

You also need to be careful when using RANK if you have duplicates in your reference range. RANK assigns the same rank to duplicate values but then does not assign the next rank(s) to any value until it has skipped past the number of duplicates.

So if I have the numbers 1, 2, 2, 3, 4 they would be ranked 1, 2, 2, 4, 5 or 5, 3, 3, 2, 1 depending on the rank order I specify. See how there are two ranks of 2 in that first example and two ranks of 3 in that second example? And how Excel skipped the rank of 3 in the first example and the rank of 4 in the second example?

(If you have a tie like this the help text for the function gives a correction factor you can use. Or if you have Excel 2013 RANK.AVG will average the ranks that would've been assigned to the tied values and return the average instead of the best rank.)

THE RANK.EQ FUNCTION

Notation: RANK.EQ(number, ref, [order])
Excel Definition: Returns the rank of a number in a list of numbers: its size relative to other values in the list; if more than one value has the same rank, the top rank of that set of values is returned.

RANK.EQ is one of the two functions that replaced RANK in Excel 2013. It works just like RANK.

Your first input is the number that needs ranked, the next input is the range to use as the reference range, and the final input tells Excel whether to evaluate rank based on ascending order or descending order.

If there's a tie and more than one value should have the same rank they will all be assigned the top rank and Excel will skip that number of ranks before assigning the next rank.

THE RANK.AVG FUNCTION

Notation: RANK.AVG(number, ref, [order])
Excel Definition: Returns the rank of a number in a list of numbers: its size relative to other values in the list; if more than one value has the same rank, the average rank is returned.

RANK.AVG is one of the two functions that replaced RANK in Excel 2013.

If there are no ties, it works just like RANK. If there are ties, RANK.AVG displays the average of the ranks that would have been assigned to those values.

Your first input is the number that needs ranked, the next input is the range to use as the reference range, and the final input tells Excel whether to evaluate rank based on ascending order or descending order.

With RANK.AVG if there is a tie in ranking, so two or more values have the same rank, Excel will return the average rank for that range of values.

So, for example:

If I have 1, 1, 1, 2, 2 in Cells A1:A5 and I want to know what the rank for a value of 1 is,

$$=RANK.AVG(1,A1:A5,1)$$

will return a value of 2.

That is because there are three values for 1 and they are ranked 1st, 2nd, and 3rd, respectively. The average of those ranks $(1+2+3)/3$ is 2.

If I have 0, 1, 1, 1, 2, 2 in Cells A1:A5 and I again use =RANK.AVG(1,A1:A5,1) this will return a value of 3 because the rank for the 1's is 2nd, 3rd, and 4th, and the average of those ranks $(2+3+4)/3$ is 3.

Compare this to RANK.EQ which would return a value of 1 in the first instance and a value of 2 in the second instance.

Here is an example of all three options side-by-side, showing the ascending and descending rank options for each using a reference range that contains 1, 2, 2, 3, and 4.

	A	B	C	D	E	F	G	H	I	J
1	REF RANGE		(0) RANK (1)			(0) RANK.EQ (1)			(0) RANK.AVG (1)	
2	1		5	1		5	1		5	1
3	2		3	2		3	2		3.5	2.5
4	2		3	2		3	2		3.5	2.5
5	3		2	4		2	4		2	4
6	4		1	5		1	5		1	5
7		Cell C2	=RANK($A2,$A$2:$A$6,0)		Cell F2	=RANK.EQ($A2,$A$2:$A$6,0)		Cell I2	=RANK.AVG($A2,$A$2:$A$6,0)	
8		Cell D2	=RANK($A2,$A$2:$A$6,1)		Cell G2	=RANK.EQ($A2,$A$2:$A$6,1)		Cell J2	=RANK.AVG($A2,$A$2:$A$6,1)	

THE SMALL FUNCTION

Notation: SMALL(array, k)

Excel Definition: Returns the k-th smallest value in a data set. For example, the fifth smallest number.

The SMALL function is pretty straight-forward. The first input is the cell range you want to use and the second input is a number representing the position in the range you're interested in.

So if you want the smallest value in a column (and didn't want to use MIN for some reason), you could use =SMALL(A:A,1) to return it.

You could also return the largest value in the range if you know the total size of the range (n) by using that value for your k value. (The ROWS function will let you count the number of rows in a range.)

THE LARGE FUNCTION

Notation: LARGE(array, k)
Excel Definition: Returns the k-th largest value in a data set. For example, the fifth largest number.

The LARGE function is the counterpart to the SMALL function. The first input is the cell range you want to use and the second input is a number representing the position in the range you're interested in.

So if you want the largest value in a column (and didn't want to use MAX for some reason), you could use =LARGE(A:A,1) to return it.

You could also return the smallest value in the range if you know the total size of the range (n) by using that value for your k value.

OTHER FUNCTIONS

That's it for this guide to functions. There are many, many more functions in Excel. The initial list of potential functions I was going to cover was about 125 functions long and I don't think that was even half of the available functions.

But as you can see after having read this guide, even within the top fifty functions things start to get pretty specialized. I'd expect if you read through this entire list from start to finish that there were a good dozen you thought you'll never use.

And chances are there's at least one I didn't cover here that you will.

So don't think this was a comprehensive listing of all Excel functions. It was just the tip of the iceberg. But hopefully it was enough coverage of Excel functions for you to now feel comfortable with how they work and for you to be able to take a different function from the ones I covered and use it successfully. (Remember if you get stuck that the Excel Help screen for each function is worth reading.)

I hope it also showed you the potential power and breadth of Excel. It's a tremendous program that can do so, so much. (You don't have to master all of it, though, to get value from it, so don't feel like you have to keep digging and digging if what you already know now meets your needs.)

Next I'm going to talk briefly about how to combine functions within a formula, something we've touched on in the examples but that I wanted to call out specifically, and then we'll discuss the various error messages and what they mean and what to do when your formula isn't working.

COMBINING FUNCTIONS

The functions we discussed in this guide are powerful in their own right. I love IF functions (even if it seems no one else does) and CONCATENATE and SUMIFS. But where the real power of Excel can come into play is when you combine functions.

So let's say I want to use CONCATENATE on a set of name data. I have columns for First Name, Middle Name, Last Name, and Suffix. And as we've already seen I could join those together to create one name entry with something like: =CONCATENATE(A2," ",B2," ",C2," ",D2) right?

But as we also discussed earlier, if someone doesn't have a middle name or a suffix I'm going to end up with extra spaces in there that I don't want and don't need. Now I could use CONCATENATE in one column and then use TRIM in another.

Or...

I could simply use =TRIM(CONCATENATE(A2," ",B2," ",C2," ",D2)) and trim my text at the same time I'm joining it together. See how easy that is? You just put the second function, CONCATENATE, in where you'd normally have a cell reference.

So if you find yourself using multiple columns to perform multiple steps maybe see if you can instead combine those steps into one.

(And if you're doing calculations and facing a significant file size issue and are using Excel 2013 or later, you might want to explore array formulas which we encountered with MODE.MULT. This is not my area of expertise, but from the little I read about them it appears they can save a lot of file space for repetitive calculations.)

WHEN THINGS GO WRONG

So we've walked through the fifty most useful functions I could identify in Excel. And now you're going to try to use them. And chances are you're going to run into some errors. I certainly do when I use functions.

You might see a #/DIV0! or a #REF! or a #VALUE! or a #N/A or a #NUM! error. It happens. Sometimes you'll realize exactly what you did, but at other times it's going to be a puzzle.

So let's me see if I can't help a bit.

#REF!

If you see #REF! in a cell it's probably because you just deleted a value that that cell was referencing. So if you had =A1+B1+C1+D1 in a cell (and I do have something similar to this in my budget worksheet), and then you deleted Column C that would create a #REF! error. Excel won't adjust the formula and drop the missing value, it will return this error message instead.

To see where the cell generating the error was in your formula, double-click in the cell with the #REF! message. This will show you the formula, including a #REF! where the missing cell used to be.

So you'll see something like =A1+B1+#REF!+D1 and you'll know that the cell you deleted was used as the third entry in that formula. If it's something like the example I just gave you where you just need to delete that cell reference, do so. Turn it into =A1+B1+D1. But you may also realize that your formula now needs to reference a different cell. If so, replace the #REF! with that cell reference. Hit enter when you've made your changes and you're done.

(This is also a good time for using Ctrl +Z if you thought you were deleting a blank cell and didn't realize it was being used in a formula and are okay with bringing that cell back.)

#VALUE!

According to Excel, a #VALUE! error means you typed your formula wrong or you're referencing a cell that's the wrong type of cell.

If you're using dates, see if the date is left-aligned. If it is, then chances are Excel is treating the date as a text entry not a date entry. That means subtraction won't work on it.

Same with numbers. If you use SUM and get this error on a range of numbers make sure that they're formatted as numbers and not text. (This shouldn't be a common problem, but could be if you've imported a data file from elsewhere.)

It can also mean that you have non-standard regional settings and that your minus sign is being used as a list separator (rather than the more standard, at least in the U.S., comma).

Or it can mean that you're referencing a data source that is no longer available like another workbook that was moved.

#DIV/0!

This is a common error to see if you've written a formula that requires division. If I input the formula =A1/B1 and there are no values in Cells A1 and B1, Excel will return #DIV/0!

You need a numeric value for your denominator to stop this from happening. (The numerator can be blank, but not the denominator.)

I usually use IF functions to suppress the #DIV/0! when I have a data table where values haven't been inputted yet. So I'll write something like =IF(B1>0,A1/B1,"").

Just be sure if you do that that the IF condition makes sense for your data. (In the example I just gave, any negative number would also result in a blank cell.)

#N/A

According to Excel, a #N/A error means that Excel isn't finding what it was asked to look for. In other words, there's no solution. This occurs most often with the VLOOKUP, HLOOKUP, LOOKUP, and MATCH functions. You tell it to look for a value in your table and that value isn't in your table.

This can be valuable information that perhaps points to a weakness in your data or your function. For example, it could indicate that the data in your lookup table is in a different format from the data in your analysis table. Or that there are extra spaces in the entries in one or the other table

But if you know this is going to happen and don't want to see the #N/A in your results, you can use the IFERROR function to suppress that result and replace it with a zero, a blank space, or even text. Just be careful, because IFERROR will replace all error messages and that may not be what you want.

#NUM!

According to Excel, you will see this error when there are numeric values in a formula or function that aren't valid. The example Excel gives involves using $1,000 in a formula instead of 1000, but when I just tried this to validate it Excel wouldn't even allow me to use that formula, it wanted to fix the formula for me as soon as I hit Enter. So this may be more of an issue in older versions of Excel.

Excel will also return this error message if an iterative function can't find a result or if the result that would be returned by the formula is too large or too small. (If you're running into this error for those reasons chances are you're doing some pretty advanced things, so we're not going to worry about that here.)

Circular References

Excel will also flag for you any time that you write a formula that references itself. (I do this on occasion without meaning to.) For example, if in Cell A5 you type =SUM(A1:A5), when you hit Enter Excel will display a dialogue box that says "Careful, we found one or more circular references in your workbook that might cause your formulas to calculate incorrectly."

Say OK and then go back to the cell with the formula and fix the issue.

Keep in mind that sometimes a circular reference error can be generated by an indirect circular reference, so you're referencing a cell that's referencing another cell and it's that other cell that's the issue.

If you can't figure out the cause and Excel doesn't "helpfully" start drawing connections on your worksheet to show it to you, in newer versions of Excel you can go to the Formulas tab and under Formula Auditing click on Trace Precedents to see what values are feeding that cell.

(Usually when this happens I know exactly what I did and it's just a matter of getting Excel to stop trying to fix it for me so I can make the correction myself. YMMV.)

Too Few Arguments

I also on occasion will try to use a function and get a warning message that I've used too few arguments for the function. When that happens check that you've included enough inputs for the function to work. Anything listed that isn't in brackets is required. So =RANDBETWEEN(bottom, top) requires that you enter values for both bottom and top but =CONCATENATE(text1, [text2],…) only requires one input.

If that's not the issue make sure that you have each of the inputs separated by commas and that your quotation marks, if there are any, are in the right places.

General Wonkiness

Sometimes everything seems fine but the formula just doesn't seem to be giving the right answer. If it's a complex formula, break it down into its components and make sure that each component works on a standalone basis.

You can also double-click on the cell for a formula and Excel will color code each of the separate components that are feeding the formula and also highlight those cells in your worksheet. Confirm that the highlighted cells are the ones you want.

For formulas you copied, verify that none of your cell ranges or cell references needed to be locked down but weren't. (I do this one often.) If you don't use $ to lock your cell references, they will adjust according to where you copied that formula. If that's what you wanted, great. If it isn't, fix it by going back to the first cell and using the $ signs to lock the cell references or by changing the cell references in the location you copied the formula to so that it works.

And, as we've seen here, sometimes there are choices you can make with a function that impact the outcome. So the value RANK will return depends on whether you tell Excel to look at your data in ascending or descending order. If you're working with a function you're not familiar with, open the Excel Help for the function and read through it. If that doesn't help, go to the website. If that doesn't help, do an Internet search to see if someone else has had the same issue.

CONCLUSION

That's it for this guide. There are many more functions that I did not cover here. Excel is incredibly broad in what it can do, but also incredibly specialized at times.

If you can think of it, chances are there's a way to do it in Excel. So don't be afraid to go to Insert Function and poke around to see what's possible.

(And if there isn't a function for what you want, you can always learn how to write your own macros in Excel. Although be careful with those. And don't look to me for that one.)

There are some more advanced aspects to working with formulas and functions in Excel that I didn't cover here or brushed past. Things like named ranges and array formulas. If you want to learn about those, start with the Excel Help function and go from there.

I find that I take things past the basic level when I need to do something specific, so I go looking for that solution that I need. If you want to be more systematic about it, there are definitely exhaustive guides out there that will cover everything for you.

And if you have a specific issue or question, feel free to reach out to me. mlhumphreywriter@gmail.com. I'm happy to help. I don't check that daily, but I do check it often and will reply.

I hope this was helpful for you. Good luck with it! Remember, save your raw data in one place, work on it in another, take your time, check the individual components of complex formulas, check your threshold cases, and Ctrl + Z (Undo) is your friend.

APPENDIX A: CELL NOTATION

If you're going to work with functions in Excel, then you need to understand how Excel references cells.

Cells are referenced based upon their column and their row. So Cell A1 is the cell in Column A and Row 1. Cell B10 is the cell in Column B and Row 10. Cell BC25232 is the cell in Column BC and in Row 25232.

If you want to reference more than one cell or cell range in a function then you can do so in a couple of ways. To reference separate and discrete cells, you list each one and you separate them with a comma. So (A1, A2, A3) refers to Cells A1, A2, and A3.

When cells are touching you can instead reference them as a single range using the colon. So (A1:A3) also refers to Cells A1, A2, and A3. Think of the colon as a "through".

You don't have to limit this to a single row or column either. You can reference A1:B25. That refers to all of the cells between Cell A1 and Cell B25. That would be all cells in Column A from Cell A1 through Cell A25 as well as all cells in Column B from Cell B1 through Cell B25.

When you note a range the left-hand cell that you list (A1) is the top left-most cell of the range and the right-hand cell you list (B25) is the bottom right-most cell of the range.

You can also reference an entire column by just using the letter and leaving off any numbers. So C:C refers to all cells in Column C.

And you can do the same for a row by leaving off the letter. So 10:10 refers to all the cells in Row 10.

If you ever reference a cell in another worksheet or another workbook, this also needs to be addressed through cell notation.

For a cell in another worksheet, you put the sheet name as it appears on the worksheet tab followed by an exclamation point before the cell reference. So Sheet1!B1 is Cell B1 in the worksheet labeled Sheet 1.

For another workbook you put the name of the workbook in brackets before the worksheet name. So [Book1]Sheet2!$D$2 refers to Cell D2 in the worksheet labeled Sheet 2 in the workbook titled Book 1.

(I should note here that I think it's a bad idea to reference data in another workbook due to the odds that the formula/function will break as soon as that other workbook is renamed or moved to a new location and that I generally don't think it's worth doing.)

Now, before you start to panic and think you need to remember all of this and that you never will, take a deep breath. Because when you're writing a formula you can simply click on the cells you need when you need them and Excel will write the cell notation for you.

It's just useful to know how this works in case something doesn't work right. (And even then you can still use Excel to show you what each cell reference is referring to. Just double-click on the formula and Excel will color code the cell references in the formula and put a matching colored border around the cells in your worksheet.)

ALPHABETICAL LISTING OF FUNCTIONS COVERED

AND	103		NA	111
AVERAGE	25		NOW	93
AVERAGEA	27		OR	105
AVERAGEIF	67		PRODUCT	21
AVERAGEIFS	69		PROPER	75
CONCATENATE	85		RAND	113
COUNT	53		RANDBETWEEN	115
COUNTA	55		RANK	117
COUNTBLANK	57		RANK.AVG	121
COUNTIF	59		RANK.EQ	119
COUNTIFS	61		RIGHT	79
FALSE	109		ROUND	47
IF	95		ROUNDDOWN	51
LARGE	125		ROUNDUP	49
LEFT	77		SMALL	123
LOWER	73		SUM	19
MAX	43		SUMIF	63
MAXA	45		SUMIFS	65
MEDIAN	29		SUMPRODUCT	23
MID	81		TEXT	87
MIN	39		TODAY	91
MINA	41		TRIM	83
MODE	31		TRUE	107
MODE.MULT	35		UPPER	71
MODE.SNGL	33		VLOOKUP	99

ABOUT THE AUTHOR

M.L. Humphrey is a former stockbroker with a degree in Economics from Stanford and an MBA from Wharton who has spent close to twenty years as a regulator and consultant in the financial services industry.

You can reach M.L. at mlhumphreywriter@gmail.com or at mlhumphrey.com.

Made in the USA
Middletown, DE
02 August 2018